Interpersonal Psychotherapy for Posttraumatic Stress Disorder

Interpersonal Psychotherapy for Posttraumatic Stress Disorder

JOHN C. MARKOWITZ

OXFORD
UNIVERSITY PRESS

OXFORD
UNIVERSITY PRESS

Oxford University Press is a department of the University of Oxford. It furthers
the University's objective of excellence in research, scholarship, and education
by publishing worldwide. Oxford is a registered trade mark of Oxford University
Press in the UK and certain other countries.

Published in the United States of America by Oxford University Press
198 Madison Avenue, New York, NY 10016, United States of America.

Library of Congress Cataloging-in-Publication Data
Names: Markowitz, John C., 1954- author.
Title: Interpersonal psychotherapy for posttraumatic stress disorder / John C. Markowitz.
Description: Oxford ; New York : Oxford University Press, [2017] |
Includes bibliographical references and index. | Description based on print version record
and CIP data provided by publisher; resource not viewed.
Identifiers: LCCN 2016019641 (print) | LCCN 2016018958 (ebook) |
ISBN 9780190465612 (ebook) | ISBN 9780190465599 (alk. paper)
Subjects: | MESH: Stress Disorders, Post-Traumatic—therapy | Psychotherapy—methods |
Interpersonal Relations | Stress Disorders, Post-Traumatic—psychology
Classification: LCC RC552.P67 (print) | LCC RC552.P67 (ebook) | NLM WM 172.5 |
DDC 616.85/21—dc23
LC record available at https://lccn.loc.gov/2016019641

9 8 7 6 5 4 3 2 1

Printed by Webcom Inc., Canada

CONTENTS

Acknowledgments vii
Introduction ix

 1. Is Exposure Therapy Necessary to Treat PTSD? 1

 2. The Target Diagnosis: PTSD 27

 3. A Pocket Guide to IPT 36

 4. Adapting IPT for PTSD 47

 5. IPT for PTSD—Initial Phase 56

 6. IPT for PTSD—Middle Phase 68

 7. IPT for PTSD—Role Transitions 79

 8. IPT for PTSD—Grief 99

 9. IPT for PTSD—Role Disputes 106

10. IPT for PTSD—Termination Phase and Maintenance 125

11. Difficult Situations and Special Circumstances 130

12. Practical Issues 138

13. Training in IPT for PTSD 142

14. Conclusion: Where Do We Go from Here? 145

Appendix: Patient Handout for IPT-PTSD 147
References 151
About the Author 159
Index 161

ACKNOWLEDGMENTS

I would like to thank many people: Gerald L. Klerman, M.D., and Myrna M. Weissman, Ph.D., who developed Interpersonal Psychotherapy and encouraged my researching this powerful treatment. Kathryn Bleiberg, Ph.D., who worked with me on the initial adaptation of IPT for PTSD at Cornell Medical Center (and who contributes a case history to Chapter 7). Randall Marshall, M.D., without whom the National Institute of Mental Health would never have funded our randomized PTSD trial. The many members of the Psychotherapies for Chronic PTSD treatment team at New York State Psychiatric Institute/Columbia University, without whom the research supporting this book could never have been accomplished; in particular, Libby Graf, Ph.D.; Hayley Pessin, Ph.D.; and Alexandra Klein Rafaeli, Psy.D., the study IPT therapists who used an earlier version of this manual. Eva Petkova, Ph.D., now at New York University School of Medicine, without whom the grant would never have been funded or analyzed. My supportive, thoughtful, and helpful colleagues at the Anxiety Disorders Clinic at New York State Psychiatric Institute, where the study took place. The National Institute of Mental Health, for funding the study (R01 MH079078). A string of mentors and colleagues too long to recount. Barbara Milrod, M.D., for her tireless help, informal editing, and support. Sarah Harrington, who championed the book at Oxford in the face of some concerns by reviewers. And, of course, the patients who came to our study for treatment of PTSD, and who benefitted from IPT and the other two study treatments, Prolonged Exposure and Relaxation Therapy.

—John C. Markowitz, M.D.

INTRODUCTION

In the midst of life, tragedy strikes. Upsetting things occur in people's lives, and they have an emotional impact. Mostly we roll with the punches: we may feel upset or worry for a few days; our sleep or appetite or concentration may briefly suffer. But for the most part, we bounce back: people are resilient. Although most individuals will experience some major trauma in the course of their lives (Kessler et al., 1995; Breslau et al., 1998), most will not develop serious psychiatric sequelae.

Some individuals have greater vulnerability to upset than others, based upon their genetic makeup and early life experience—including early life trauma. Some individuals experience greater life difficulties than others. Some life events are sufficiently horrific that the American Psychiatric Association (APA) *Diagnostic and Statistical Manual of Mental Disorders* (DSM) deems them "trauma"—a term that has undergone multiple redefinitions. In the current *DSM-5* (2013), the definition is:

> Exposure to actual or threatened death, serious injury, or sexual violence in one (or more) of the following ways:
>
> 1. Directly experiencing the traumatic event(s).
> 2. Witnessing, in person, the event(s) as it occurred to others.
> 3. Learning that the traumatic event(s) occurred to a close family member or close friend [. . .].
> 4. Experiencing repeated or extreme exposure to aversive details of the traumatic event(s) (e.g., first responders collecting human remains; police officers repeatedly exposed to details of child abuse). (APA, 2013)

After experiencing such an event, most people still show resilience, but some 3.5% of people annually (Kessler, Chiu et al., 2005) and 6.8% over a lifetime (Kessler, Berglund, et al., 2005) will be unable to shake it off. Rates are still higher in military personnel (Wisco et al., 2014; in press) and other high-risk groups. The traumatic experience stays with them: they can't get it out of their minds; they relive the event continually, involuntarily. At the same time, the story may seem overwhelming, fragmented, hard to put together. Everything reminds them of the trauma: the weather, smells, sounds, particular objects, places, etc. The trauma affects their sleep and mood. They feel overly emotional, or alternatively numb. They withdraw socially. Their sense of safety is shattered: the world feels like a bewildering and menacing minefield, and the people in it, untrustworthy. At such a point we begin to think about posttraumatic stress disorder (PTSD).

Example: Amy, a 37-year-old, married, white, Catholic businesswoman and mother of one, presented for treatment after having been robbed at knifepoint on a dark street eight months before. She described recurrent flashbacks to this frightening event, in which she lost her purse but also feared for her life. She reported trouble falling asleep, waking to nightmares, poor concentration, and high distractibility. Her mood was anxious and somewhat depressed. She tried to avoid thinking about the event, yet almost everything reminded her of it: the neighborhood where she was robbed, similar streets, sharp objects, the tone of people's voices, smells from the street, darkness. There were aspects of the event she had blocked out or couldn't piece together.
Amy had also begun to fear contact with people and with the environment. Previously gregarious, she no longer went out at night, and even minimized leaving home by day. Her work suffered. She no longer wanted to travel for business, fearing contact with strangers. She felt helpless, mistrustful, confused, and empty. She no longer spoke to her boyfriend or to friends or family. She also reported that in childhood she had been physically abused by her mother.

PTSD is a widespread (Kessler, Chiu, et al., 2005), painful, debilitating (McMillen et al., 2002; Sareen et al., 2007), often chronic, and even lethal disorder (Sareen et al., 2007). Thankfully, it's treatable. Several treatments have been tested in randomized controlled clinical trials and shown to benefit patients, reducing PTSD symptoms and improving social functioning and quality of life. The dominant treatment approach for PTSD in recent decades has been Cognitive Behavioral Therapy (CBT), which can take several forms. All of the variants have focused on the principle of fear-habituation and fear-extinction, and on the practical clinical approach of exposing patients to the traumatic memories they most fear, asking them to face the fears that reminders of their trauma evoke. This initially makes people more anxious, but if they face their fears rather than avoiding them, they can realize that the danger is behind them. They *habituate*: they get used to facing their fear, and the fear subsides. With practice, someone who witnessed a fatal train wreck can get used to riding in trains again, realizing: "That was then, this is now. The danger has passed, and its memories are not dangerous." Individuals may still have a very unpleasant memory of the traumatic event, but it need not affect their anxiety level or behavior.

These treatments, mostly cognitive behavioral in format (Foa et al., 2000), work very well for many patients. Like all psychiatric and psychological (and medical) treatments, however, exposure-based cognitive behavioral treatments are imperfect: they don't benefit everyone. Some patients who might benefit from an exposure-based approach are understandably too frightened to face their worst fears, and refuse to try one.

This book addresses an alternative to the fear-extinction model. We tested Interpersonal Psychotherapy (IPT), a very different kind of psychotherapy that, like CBT, has been shown to benefit patients with major depression and with eating disorders, as a treatment for patients with chronic PTSD. IPT is not an exposure-based therapy. In a randomized controlled study, we found IPT was essentially equivalent to Prolonged Exposure, the best-proven exposure-based CBT treatment, in reducing PTSD symptoms (Markowitz et al., 2015). Moreover, IPT had some advantages among PTSD patients who were also depressed. IPT is based on interpersonal principles: on helping benumbed patients to regain emotional awareness and to use their rediscovered emotions to handle interpersonal encounters, building social skills to determine whom to trust, how to defend themselves against the untrustworthy, and how to mobilize trustworthy social support.

When tragedy strikes, how we survive it may depend not only upon our genetic makeup, prior traumas, and degree of exposure to the traumatic event, but also on interpersonal factors, such as our social skills and social support. Who we are as social beings matters in our response to tragedy and trauma. Our study results have prompted interest in this interpersonal approach—IPT for PTSD—among both clinicians and patients. This book is intended to address that growing interest.

This book began as a research treatment manual for the therapists in our study. In expanding it for publication, I struggled with the tension between retaining the flavor of a research manual and toning down its technical rigor. Most research psychotherapy manuals are technical, expecting therapists to already have experience with the treatment techniques and its jargon. Most popular books make no such assumptions. I have aimed, successfully or not, for a compromise: trying not to write in jargon, but preserving the sense of research rigor. I hope that readers of this book will include both research therapists in treatment trials (our study requires replication!) and general clinicians who have no intention of conducting formal research.

For the latter readers, this book should at times provide a peek into how psychotherapy research proceeds. This will be most evident in Chapter 1, which supplies the research background that validates the IPT treatment approach for PTSD, and in Chapter 12, which presents prescriptions and proscriptions for research therapists. Readers not interested in heavy data or research limits can skip these sections, but should know that the data are there.

Interpersonal Psychotherapy for Posttraumatic Stress Disorder

Is Exposure Therapy Necessary to Treat PTSD?

Security is mostly a superstition. . . . Avoiding danger
is no safer in the long run than outright exposure.
—HELEN KELLER, *The Open Door (1957)*

Before we jump into Interpersonal Psychotherapy (IPT) as a treatment for
posttraumatic stress disorder (PTSD), it's helpful to have a clinical and a research context. This chapter describes the state of accepted treatments for
PTSD, the dominant theory and rationale supporting exposure therapy as a
treatment, and the rationale and evidence for IPT as a treatment alternative.

EXPOSURE

A large body of randomized controlled clinical trials shows that exposure
therapy, which exposes patients to reminders that evoke their traumas in order
to extinguish excessive fears, benefits many patients with PTSD. Almost all
empirically tested psychotherapies for PTSD have relied on exposure techniques, dating back to Kardiner and Spiegel's (1947) treatment of World War II
veterans. Treatments like Prolonged Exposure (Foa et al., 1991), Cognitive
Processing Therapy (Resick et al., 2008), Eye Movement Desensitization and
Reprocessing (EMDR; Shapiro, 2001), and other treatments, mostly variants of
Cognitive Behavioral Therapy (CBT), all rely on helping patients face triggers
of frightening memories and experiences they avoid. (Cognitive Processing
Therapy has also shown benefit sans its exposure component [Resick et al., 2008].)

This exposure to trauma reminders, initially anxiety-provoking but taking place in a safe setting with a reassuring therapist, leads patients to recognize that the reminders themselves are not inherently dangerous just because of their association with a traumatic event. Patients may long have avoided stimuli like physical settings (e.g., tall buildings, airplanes, and downtown Manhattan, for World Trade Center survivors), smells, colors, or objects associated with the trauma. In treatment, they come to realize, through exposure, that this avoidance need not continue, and it need not interfere with their lives.

Exposure-based treatment is founded on very old behavioral principles: the more you fear something, the more you avoid it. Moreover, the more you avoid something, the more dangerous it seems, and the more you then fear it. This vicious cycle leads individuals to avoid a host of potential triggering stimuli, which avoidance constricts their lives. They live in fear of fear, avoiding large areas of experience because, following a trauma, nothing really feels safe.

If a therapist can induce a patient to confront a reminder of a trauma and face it, fear initially rises but then subsides as the patient has a chance to reevaluate the trauma reminder (Foa & Kozak, 1986). This habituation lowers anxiety with each subsequent exposure, and may eventually extinguish the fear. Exposure therapists help patients construct a hierarchy of fears, ranging from mild to severe, and start with the milder ones, building up to the seemingly most dangerous. In Prolonged Exposure therapy, therapists tape the 90-minute exposure sessions and send patients home to review the latest session tape every day for the remainder of the week. Thus therapy consists of 90-minute daily imaginal exposure. In addition, patients undergo *in vivo* exposures; for example, returning to Ground Zero if the trauma involved the World Trade Center. Again, the principle is that, by facing reminders of your trauma, you can recognize that the triggering stimulus is not the trauma and can come to appreciate that fear reminders are not inherently dangerous. By the end of treatment, by repeatedly recounting the trauma and confronting its reminders, a patient ideally has constructed a seamless history of the traumatic incident(s), and has faced and become habituated to related fears.

Bolstering this behavioral fear-extinction paradigm, research studies have located a fear-extinction circuit in the brain. Individuals with PTSD have overactive amygdalas; neuroimaging studies have shown that behavioral treatment strengthens "top-down" control by the prefrontal cortex, in effect subduing amygdalar activity (Rauch et al., 2006). Unlike the ego, id, and superego, then, the fear-behavior circuit has a definable neuroanatomical locus.

In recognition of this impressive clinical and physiological/neuroanatomical research, treatment guidelines have unanimously endorsed exposure-based treatments as first-line interventions for PTSD. The American Psychiatric

Association (APA) treatment guidelines for PTSD state: "The shared element [among efficacious treatments] of controlled exposure may be the critical intervention" (APA, 2004). The United Kingdom National Institute for Health and Care Excellence (NICE) guidelines similarly endorse the approach: "All people with PTSD should be offered a course of trauma-focused psychological treatment (trauma-focused cognitive behavioural therapy [CBT] or eye movement desensitisation and reprocessing [EMDR])" (NICE, 2005). The Institute of Medicine (IOM) recommended *only* exposure-based treatment, finding too little evidence to support pharmacotherapy of PTSD (IOM, 2008)—even though research indicates that treatment with serotonin reuptake inhibitors does benefit patients with PTSD (e.g., Brady et al., 2000; Marshall et al., 2001; Schneier et al., 2012).

Is exposure a necessary ingredient for treatment? Its necessity has in recent years become a near dogma in the field. Perhaps not since the heyday of psychoanalysis has a theory so dominated a field as exposure-based theory does the psychotherapy of anxiety disorders today. (Research showing that Cognitive Processing Therapy minus its narrative exposure component does benefit patients with PTSD [Resick et al., 2008] has not changed the overall perspective of the field.) Exposure-based treatment does work, but—like all treatments for all conditions—it has limitations. Exposure therapy is difficult work that can be painful for patients and clinicians. Some patients (and therapists) refuse to do it, and the dropout rate is high: roughly 30% across studies (Hembree et al., 2003). Patients with high levels of dissociation may have poor outcomes, as their detachment may make it difficult for their exposure sessions to sink in (Lanius et al., 2010). Ninety-minute sessions may be difficult to incorporate into clinic practice. Despite an impressive rollout of exposure training for therapists in the Veterans Administration (VA) system, few therapists have actually been using these techniques, and dropout rates from such treatment have been high (Watts et al., 2014; Kehle-Forbes et al., 2016). So an empirically validated, non–exposure-based psychotherapy would be a valuable alternative for individuals suffering from PTSD.

ANOTHER THEORY

The fear-extinction theory makes sense for PTSD, a disorder based on a frightening traumatic event and characterized by anxiety and avoidance. Yet that vantage is not the only possible perspective. Posttraumatic stress disorder also has numerous interpersonal features (Markowitz et al., 2009).

The *DSM-IV* (*Diagnostic and Statistical Manual*, 4th edition) PTSD avoidance symptom cluster included descriptions of patients avoiding "conversations" and "people" that evoke traumatic memories. Individuals may feel "detach[ed] or estrange[d] from others," show "restricted range of affect," or have "irritability or outbursts of anger" in interpersonal contexts. "Diminished interest or participation in significant activities" occurs in social settings. Prime *DSM-IV* examples of a perceived foreshortened future are social: "career, marriage, children" (APA, 1994, p. 428). The *DSM-5* (5th ed.) revision has retained many of these interpersonal descriptions, despite a growing emphasis on cognitive factors in its text (APA, 2013, pp. 274–279).

The PTSD clinical literature describes a variety of associated interpersonal features. Patients become withdrawn, mistrustful, affect-dysregulated, and "interpersonally hypervigilant" (Bleiberg & Markowitz, 2005) in social circumstances: they mistrust not only their environment, but the people in it. PTSD compromises emotional and social intimacy with others (Riggs et al., 1998), burdens the significant others surrounding individuals with PTSD (Beckham et al., 1996), and impairs social and marital functioning (Cloitre et al., 1997; Amaya-Jackson et al., 1999; North et al., 1999; Liang et al., 2006, pp. 26–29). Individuals with PTSD may fall into maladaptive interpersonal patterns that increase the risk of revictimization (Davidson et al., 1991; Cloitre et al., 1997; Liang et al., 2006).

What Do the Data Show?

Although interpersonal aspects are prominent features of PTSD, this does not necessarily mean that focusing on them in therapy will benefit patients with PTSD. Nonetheless, a sparse (if growing) body of research has begun to test the effects of an interpersonal approach (Markowitz, Lipsitz, & Milrod, 2014). A few small open trials of IPT have mostly suggested some benefits to patients (see Table 1.1).

Yet open trials carry limited weight: they do not control for the passage of time or for the non-specific effects of meeting with a caring therapist. Randomized clinical trials control for such factors, and there have now been two randomized controlled trials of IPT for patients with chronic PTSD.

Krupnick et al. Study. The first controlled IPT study, conducted by Janice Krupnick and colleagues (2008), treated 48 chronically and severely traumatized women, mostly minorities and mostly low-income, recruited from public gynecology and family health clinics in the Washington, D.C., area. These women were seeking treatment for other medical conditions, not for PTSD or other psychiatric diagnoses. IPT was conducted in a group format, capitalizing on the potential for patients to support one another, to realize that they were not alone in having been assaulted or abused. The

Table 1.1. STUDIES OF IPT FOR CHRONIC PTSD

Study	Design	IPT	Adaptation	Outcome	Remarks and Effect Sizes
Bleiberg & Markowitz, 2005	Open trial $n = 14$	14 weekly sessions	Exposure to trauma reminders prohibited	Pre/post CAPS $67 \to 25$ Attrition: 7%	Large effect sizes: CAPS d = 1.8
Robertson et al., 2007	Open trial $n = 13$	8 weekly group IPT sessions	"Specially prepared" treatment manual(?); standard group IPT?	"Modest" IES improvement Attrition: 0%	Results stable on 3-month f/u; ES: IES subscales $r = 0.63–0.67$
Ray & Webster, 2010	Open trial $n = 9$	8 weekly 2-hour group IPT sessions	Based on group IPT manual (Wilfley et al., 2000)	IES significantly improved $(p < .05)$ Attrition: 0%	Some symptomatic slippage on 2-month f/u; (ES: not calculable)
Krupnick et al., 2008	RCT: IPT vs. WL $n = 48$	16 weekly 2-hour group IPT sessions	Adapted for low-income, highly traumatized minority women	IPT > WL (CAPS, $p < .001$) Attrition: 29% IPT	Gains persisted at 4-month f/u ES: CAPS d = 1.31
Campanini et al., 2010	Open augmentation of med trial $n = 40$	16 weekly 2-hour group IPT sessions	Similar to Krupnick et al.; IPT did not focus on trauma exposure	CAPS $72 \to 37$, with large effect size (1.2) Attrition: 17%	Medication non-responders; ES: CAPS d = 1.17

CAPS = Clinician-Administered PTSD Scale; ES = effect size (Cohen's d); F/u = follow-up; IES = Impact of Events Scale; IPT = Interpersonal Psychotherapy; RCT = randomized controlled trial; WL = waiting list

SOURCE: Markowitz et al., 2014.

researchers compared group IPT to a waiting list (admittedly not the strongest comparison condition) in which patients were repeatedly evaluated but did not receive psychotherapy. Medication was held stable for those who were taking psychotropic medication.

Paired woman therapists conducted 16 two-hour IPT sessions for groups of three to five women. The women in treatment had been multiply traumatized, with an average of 6.8 (standard deviation [SD] = 4.2) interpersonal traumas (!). The authors considered the dropout rate low in the context of this high-risk, non–treatment-seeking population: 71% of patients attended at least half the sessions. On the other hand, only 63% of IPT and 44% of waiting list subjects completed symptom ratings at treatment termination, and only 81% of IPT patients and 63% of waiting list subjects were rated at four-month follow-up.

Scores on the Clinician-Administered PTSD Scale (CAPS; Blake et al., 1995; Weathers et al., 2001) fell from 65.2 (SD = 20.9) in IPT to 40.6 post treatment and 38.5 (SD = 24.4) at four month follow-up: that is, from severe symptoms to mild to moderate symptoms. The waiting list subject scores were 62.6 (SD = 16.6), 56.6 (25.1), and 41.6 (SD = 26.7) at the three time points ($p < .001$). IPT also produced significantly greater reductions on the Hamilton Depression Rating Scale (Hamilton, 1960) than did waiting list status. IPT patients improved on four of five subscales (all but Aggression) of the Inventory of Interpersonal Problems (IIP; Horowitz et al., 1988), whereas waiting list group IIP scores worsened over time.

Summary: The Krupnick study is important as the first randomized controlled trial of IPT for PTSD, and it generated interesting results. A score greater than 60 on the CAPS, where the patients started before treatment, indicates severe PTSD; a score of 40 falls right on the diagnostic threshold (Weathers et al., 2001). Thus group IPT tended not to bring about remission, but did produce clinically meaningful improvement in a repeatedly battered population. A weakness of the study is the waiting list control condition: a comparison is only as strong as its comparator, and showing that IPT was better than no treatment is not definitively impressive. Nonetheless, it's a start, a step into new comparative treatment territory. Although the five therapists in this study had some clinical experience, ranging from five to twenty years of work in group and psychodynamic psychotherapy, only one of them had had prior experience with IPT. If the therapists were not polished in delivering IPT, the results might then underestimate the potency of the treatment.

Campanini et al. Study. In a study in Brazil, Campanini and colleagues (2010) used group IPT as adjunctive therapy, adding it to the treatment of 40 patients with PTSD related to interpersonal violence who had not responded to at least 12 weeks of pharmacotherapy. As in the Krupnick and colleagues study, patients received 16 two-hour IPT sessions in groups of six to eight patients. They also received an individual session prior to starting group, at mid-treatment, and at the end of treatment. IPT focused on interpersonal issues, not on trauma exposure. Patients were maintained on steady doses of the medications, consisting mainly of antidepressants.

Thirty-three (83%) completed the study, and all had at least one outcome evaluation. CAPS scores fell from 72.3 (standard error [SE] = 4.7) to 36.5 (SE = 5.4) ($p < .001$, effect size = 1.2). There were impressive improvements across symptom clusters. Other assessments showed general improvement: the mean Beck Depression Inventory (BDI) scores fell from 26.2 (1.8) at baseline to 13.3 (1.6) ($p < .0001$, ES = 1.2), essentially from moderately severe depression to very mild depression on average. The Social Adjustment Scale (Weissman & Bothwell, 1976) improved from 2.59 (0.12) to 2.17 (0.11) ($p < .0007$, ES = 0.63).

Summary: The results of the Campanini study are very encouraging, showing that group IPT had an added effect for patients non-responsive to medication. On the other hand, this was an open trial, so the improvement cannot be determined to be specific to group IPT: without a comparison condition, it is unclear whether group IPT fared better than other added treatments might have. As a side note, the social adjustment scores are impressively impaired in this study: extremely so at the outset, and still quite impaired after treatment, despite meaningful improvement. (Lower scores are better, and 1.6 marks the normal range [Weissman & Bothwell, 1976].)

Our Open Trial. We have conducted two studies of individual IPT for PTSD. The first was an open trial—all patients received IPT—at Cornell University Medical College in New York, which we had begun even before the September 11, 2001, attack made PTSD huge news in New York City. Our reasoning in adapting IPT for PTSD was this.

1. Interpersonal Psychotherapy links patients' syndromes (for example, major depression) to important life events that either trigger or result from the psychiatric disorder. Psychiatric disorders do not occur in a vacuum, but in an interpersonal context. In extending IPT from mood and eating disorders to anxiety disorders, PTSD seemed the obvious place to start, as it is a disorder defined by a life event.

2. Because various exposure-based treatments for PTSD existed, we felt IPT should take a different approach. Never exposure-focused, IPT would not reconstruct traumatic events with patients, but would rather address *the interpersonal sequelae of having been traumatized.* Rather than reconditioning patients not to fear reminders of their trauma, IPT would help patients regain social supports and figure out whom they could trust and not trust in their social world.

3. We noticed that trauma shatters patients' sense of safety about their environment and about people in their environment. Individuals with PTSD suffer from affective distancing or numbing, and withdraw socially. Unable to trust their feelings, they cannot "read" or trust their environment. Numbed, they avoid or try to ignore painful negative affects (anger, sadness, anxiety) that in fact serve as important signals about interpersonal encounters. Without such input, patients were "flying blind" and likely to be revictimized, not knowing whom to trust and whom to avoid. Hence we decided to focus the initial stage of IPT treatment on *affective attunement*. We asked patients repeatedly how they were feeling, what the name of the feeling was ("I'm upset," for example, is non-specific), whether it was a reasonable reaction to the interpersonal encounter, and what it might tell them about that encounter. In discussing current daily interactions—not past traumatic events—we tried to help patients gain an emotional vocabulary for their interactions, to see negative emotions not as dangerous but as useful interpersonal signposts they could use to decode confusing situations.

With Kathryn Bleiberg at Cornell, I wrote the first version of the treatment manual that is the basis for this book. We somewhat arbitrarily set the length of treatment at 14 weekly 50-minute sessions. As no one had tested IPT for PTSD, we had no idea how long treatment ought to last.

Our initial open study (Bleiberg & Markowitz, 2005) treated 14 patients with chronic PTSD. Therapists used much of the first half of treatment to rebuild emotional attunement in benumbed patients—this symptom is not typical of depression, but it is a hallmark of chronic PTSD. Then therapists applied standard IPT maneuvers to patients' difficulties with trust and expressing emotions in daily relationships. Therapists avoided encouraging exposure to trauma reminders. Patients with varied, but predominantly interpersonal rather than impersonal, traumas received 14 weekly IPT sessions. All but one patient completed treatment.

At the end of treatment, 12 of 14 patients no longer met diagnostic criteria for PTSD. CAPS (Blake et al., 1995; Weathers et al., 2001) scores fell from 67 (SD = 19) to 25 (SD = 17), a large within-group effect (d = 1.8), with improvement across PTSD symptom clusters. This drop in the CAPS score took patients from severe PTSD to near-remission. Depressive symptoms, anger reactions, and social functioning improved. As patients became more comfortable with their emotions and handling daily interpersonal encounters, they exposed themselves to traumatic fear reminders without therapist encouragement—a change necessary for PTSD remission. (See Table 1.2.)

Table 1.2. CORNELL TRIAL: SCORES AT BASELINE AND AFTER 14 WEEKS OF IPT-PTSD

Assessment	Baseline		Week 14		Change	SD of Mean	Effect	p^b
	Mean	SD	Mean	SD	Mean	Change	Size[a]	
CAPS-2 (*n* = 15)	66.3	16.0	23.5	16.1	42.8	23.6	1.8	.001
PSS-SR (*n* = 16)								
Total Score	69.4	21.5	20.3	14.2	49.1	22.6	2.2	.000
Re-experiencing	20.2	6.9	6.8	5.3	13.4	7.6	1.8	.001
Avoidance	28.8	9.8	6.5	6.7	22.3	11.4	2.0	.001
Hyperarousal	21.0	7.5	7.0	5.8	13.9	7.8	1.8	.000
Ham-D (*n* = 16)	17.8	8.0	8.8	5.9	9.0	7.0	1.3	.002
BDI (*n* = 14)	16.9	8.9	6.1	6.8	10.9	9.4	1.2	.003
STAXI								
State (*n* = 15)	14.5	5.9	10.5	0.99	4.0	5.5	0.73	.005
Trait (*n* = 13)	18.5	5.0	15.3	2.9	3.1	4.4	0.70	.025
SAS-SR (*n* = 13)	2.5	0.42	1.9	0.37	0.52	0.40	1.3	.003

CAPS-2 = Clinician-Administered PTSD Scale, version 2; PSS-SR = Posttraumatic Stress Scale–Self Report Version; Ham-D = 24-item Hamilton Depression Rating Scale; BDI = Beck Depression Inventory; STAXI = State-Trait Anger Experience Inventory; SAS-SR = Social Adjustment Scale–Self Report version.

[a] Within-group effect size (Cohen's d)

[b] Wilcoxon paired-rank sum tests

Patients reported general interpersonal improvement on the Social Adjustment Scale (Weissman & Bothwell, 1976) and other interpersonal measures. Ten completed the Interpersonal Psychotherapy Outcome Scale (IPOS; Markowitz et al., 2006), a self-report measure on which patients score change in the interpersonal problem area which IPT focused on during the treatment interval. On the IPOS, 1 = significant worsening in the area, 2 = mild worsening, 3 = no change, 4 = mild improvement, and 5 = significant improvement. All subjects reported some positive interpersonal change (minimum score = 4), and mean improvement was 4.77 (SD = 0.34) out of a possible five. IPOS scores correlated with CAPS improvement: that is, how much patients improved in resolving their interpersonal difficulties correlated with reduction in PTSD symptoms (Markowitz et al., 2006).

Ten patients completed the Inventory of Interpersonal Problems (Horowitz et al., 1988), a measure of interpersonal difficulties, and showed significant improvement in total score (ES = 1.15; Wilcoxon Signed Ranks Test, *p* = 0.005) and on all subscales, particularly the Cold/Distant (ES = 1.39, p = 0.008) and Self-Sacrificing (ES = 1.38, *p* = 0.009) circumplex subscales. Compared to normative scores, interpersonal function on the IIP for PTSD subjects at baseline was worse than that of 82% of the population; after treatment, it approached the norm (54%) (Markowitz et al., 2006).

Six subjects assessed at six-month follow-up showed persisting remission, defined by a CAPS score of less than 20 (Davidson et al., p. 191). Mean CAPS score at follow-up was 16.8 (SD = 9.6), compared to 14.2 (9.8) at week 14; Posttraumatic Stress Scale–Self Report (PSS-SR, a PTSD self-report scale) mean was 20.9 (26.9) at six months, versus 12.0 (6.8) at 14 weeks.

Summary: These very encouraging findings have their limits: as noted, an open trial can provide encouragement for treatment development, but it cannot prove efficacy. Efficacy requires a randomized controlled trial. This study, however, provided the groundwork for such a trial.

Randomized Controlled Trial. With funding from the National Institute of Mental Health (NIMH), we next conducted a randomized controlled trial, comparing non-exposure IPT to both Prolonged Exposure, the gold standard and best tested exposure-based treatment, developed by Edna Foa (Foa & Rothbaum, 1998); and to Relaxation Therapy (Jacobsen, 1938), which had previously been compared to Prolonged Exposure and functioned as an active control condition. Relaxation Therapy controlled for therapist time, attention, and empathy, and it offered a different mechanism for treatment improvement: namely, progressive muscle relaxation. We designed this trial as a *non-inferiority* study, to test whether IPT would produce improvements within 15 CAPS points of Prolonged Exposure and would fare better than Relaxation Therapy. According to the developers of the CAPS (Weathers et al., 2001), a 15-point score on the CAPS constitutes a meaningful clinical difference. Based on power analyses, we therefore chose 12.5 points as a cutoff: a mean difference in CAPS change of 12.5 points or more would indicate at least minimal inferiority, and less than 12.5 points would indicate less than minimal inferiority (Markowitz et al., 2015).

Data analyses followed the intention-to-treat principle. Some participants who discontinued treatment were later assessed at the specified assessment times, whereas other participants who completed treatment missed the mid-treatment assessment. We compared patients with missing post-randomization data to those without missing data on their baseline characteristics. No comparisons between subjects with and without post-randomization assessment overall, or within treatment groups, were statistically significantly different, and no differences approached clinically meaningful magnitude. Efficacy of the three treatments with respect to symptom severity was estimated based on longitudinal mixed-effects models, using multiple imputation for the missing values. For each variable (score on the CAPS, the PSS-SR, the Hamilton Depression Rating Scale (HAM-D), the Social Adjustment Scale–Self-Report, the Quality of Life Measure, and the IIP), we used the Markov chain Monte Carlo technique to obtain a monotone missing data pattern. We then applied a predictive mean-matching regression method separately for the three treatment groups. To increase the likelihood that the missing-at-random assumption was valid, in addition to the previous values of the variable being imputed, we used all other symptom variables and baseline major depression status as predictors in predictive mean-matching regression. Fifty imputed data sets were generated.

We modeled the post-randomization values as functions of treatment, time, and their interaction, controlling for baseline values of the outcome and major depression status. If the time-by-treatment interaction reached statistical significance, differences between treatments were estimated separately at mid-treatment (week 7) and at end of treatment (week 14); otherwise, the model was refitted with only main effects for treatment and time, and the differences were assessed from a model postulating similar relationships between the treatments at all times.

Response and remission rates were estimated based on the observed data using pre-specified criteria: response was defined as a decrease of > 30% from baseline CAPS score, and remission was defined as a CAPS score of < 20 (Blake et al., 1995; Weathers et al., 2001; Davidson et al., 2002). Participants for whom these data were missing were categorized as "nonresponders" and "nonremitters." Statistical significance was assessed throughout at an alpha of 0.05 (two-sided). We reported p values without adjustment for multiple testing, as the reported results pertain to pre-specified hypotheses and tests. All analyses used Statistical Analysis Software (SAS/STAT), version 9.2.

We randomly assigned 110 patients who were not taking any psychotropic medication to 14 weeks during which they received either 14 50-minute sessions of IPT (Weissman et al., 2007), ten 90-minute sessions of Prolonged Exposure (Foa & Rothbaum, 1998), or nine 90-minute and one 30-minute session of Relaxation Therapy (Jacobsen, 1938). Treatments were run at their standard lengths, amounting to 700 minutes of IPT, 900 minutes of Prolonged Exposure, and 840 minutes of Relaxation Therapy. Figure 1.1 is a Consolidated Standards of Reporting Trials (CONSORT) diagram illustrating the flow of the study.

Therapists were trained by expert supervisors, followed treatment manuals, and conducted pilot cases to develop expertise before beginning the study. The Prolonged Exposure supervisor, Elizabeth Hembree had been involved in numerous randomized trials of Prolonged Exposure and was perhaps the primary trainer of therapists, in collaboration with Edna Foa, who invented the treatment. Karina Lovell, who had supervised therapists in two prior studies comparing Relaxation Therapy to Prolonged Exposure, supervised our

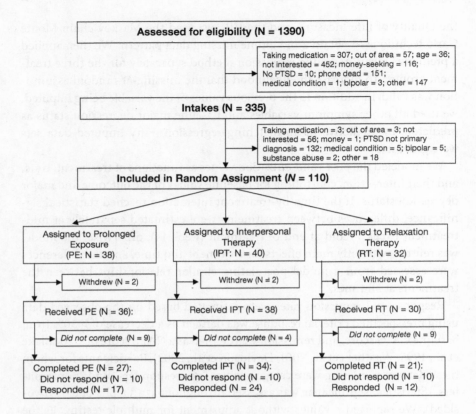

Figure 1.1. Consort diagram of study flow.

Relaxation Therapy therapists. I supervised the IPT therapists. All sessions were recorded on audiotape, and reliable, trained raters blind to treatment and session number rated a sub-sample of treatment sessions using instruments that included the best available discriminator of IPT and cognitive behavioral treatments, the Collaborative Study Psychotherapy Rating Scale (CSPRS-6; Hollon, 1984).

Study therapists were Ph.D./Psy.D. psychologists or psychiatrists, who each treated a minimum of two pilot cases to ensure their competence and adherence to treatment. The study included two Prolonged Exposure therapists experienced in a previous PTSD study (Schneier et al., 2012); four IPT therapists; and four Relaxation Therapy therapists. Therapists reported primary allegiance to their study therapy, an important guard against bias in a treatment trial (Falkenström et al., 2013). Therapy teams did not differ significantly in mean age (Prolonged Exposure 47.5 years [SD = 10.6], IPT 41.0 years [SD = 9.1], and Relaxation Therapy 34.8 years [SD = 5.1]) or in years of modality-specific psychotherapy experience (Prolonged Exposure 7.5 years [SD = 0.7], IPT 9.0 years

[SD = 8.4], and Relaxation Therapy 3.8 years [SD = 4.4]). Patients could choose male or female therapists (Markowitz et al., 2015).

The 110 study patients all had chronic PTSD and a minimum CAPS severity score of 50—indicating at least moderately severe PTSD. None was taking psychotropic medication, and outside treatment was prohibited during the 14 weeks of the trial. The patients were highly traumatized and chronically ill (Tables 1.3 and 1.4), racially and ethnically diverse, and had a mean age of 40.1 years. Only 15.5% were married or living with a partner, and only 36.4% were employed full-time (10.9% were students). Ninety-three percent reported interpersonal traumas—which tend to cause greater distress than impersonal traumas such as natural disasters (Kessler et al., 1995; Markowitz et al., 2009). More than half (58%) of patients reported chronic trauma (mean duration since primary trauma, 14.1 years [SD = 14.4]), including sexual (35%) and physical (61%) abuse. Thirty-six percent reported childhood or adolescent traumas. Three-quarters of patients had previously received psychotherapy, and nearly half had received pharmacotherapy for PTSD (Markowitz et al., 2015).

Table 1.4 describes patients' psychiatric debility. As anticipated, half had current comorbid major depression; one-third reported having had multiple depressive episodes. Nearly half met criteria for personality disorders, particularly paranoid, obsessive-compulsive, and avoidant.

Patients assigned to Prolonged Exposure attended a mean of 8.3 sessions (SD = 3.1) (a mean of 748 minutes [SD = 277] overall); IPT patients attended a mean of 12.6 sessions (SD = 3.4) (a mean of 630 minutes [SD = 69] overall); and Relaxation Therapy patients attended a mean 7.8 (SD = 3.5) sessions (a mean of 667 minutes [SD = 290] overall), or 83%, 90%, and 78% of prescribed sessions, respectively.

Outcomes

CAPS scores substantially improved in each therapy over the 14-week course of treatment (Table 1.5), with large within-group pre-treatment–post-treatment effect sizes (Cohen's d): for Prolonged Exposure, $d = 1.88$; for IPT, $d = 1.69$; and for Relaxation Therapy, $d = 1.32$. These changes indicate large reductions in PTSD symptoms in all three treatments. The time-by-treatment interaction was not significant. In comparison with Relaxation Therapy, Prolonged Exposure showed a significant advantage ($p = 0.010$), whereas IPT's advantage fell short of statistical significance ($p = 0.097$). *Crucially, the between-group difference in CAPS change scores between Prolonged Exposure and IPT was 5.5 points, less than the 12.5-point minimal inferiority threshold that we had defined* a priori. Thus the null hypothesis of more than minimal inferiority of IPT was rejected ($p = 0.035$) (Table 1.5).

Table 1.3. DEMOGRAPHIC CHARACTERISTICS OF PATIENTS WITH PTSD RECEIVING PROLONGED EXPOSURE, IPT, OR RELAXATION THERAPY

Characteristic	Prolonged Exposure (*n* = 38)		IPT (*n* = 40)		Relaxation Therapy (*n* = 32)		Overall Sample (*n* = 110)	
	Mean	SD	Mean	SD	Mean	SD	Mean	SD
Age (years)	41.76	11.99	38.12	11.21	40.62	11.48	40.10	11.57
Education (years)	15.39	2.39	15.78	2.04	16.25	1.95	15.78	2.15
	N	%	N	%	N	%	N	%
Female	21	55	28	70	28	88	77	70
Race								
White	22	58	31	78	19	59	72	65
African American	9	24	4	10	6	19	19	17
Asian or Pacific Islander	2	5	3	8	4	13	9	8
Other	5	13	2	5	3	9	10	9
Hispanic ethnicity	12	32	8	20	11	34	31	28
Marital status								
Single	26	68	28	70	19	59	73	66
Married or cohabitating	5	13	6	15	6	19	17	15
Divorced	7	18	6	15	7	22	20	18
Employment								
Full-time	14	37	12	30	14	44	40	36
Part-time	4	11	5	13	6	19	15	14
Homemaker	0	0	1	3	0	0	1	1
Student	5	13	4	10	4	13	13	12
Unemployed < 6 months	3	8	4	10	3	9	10	9
Unemployed > 6 months	8	21	10	25	4	13	22	20
Retired	0	0	1	3	0	0	1	1
Disabled	2	5	0	0	0	0	2	2
Other	2	5	3	8	1	3	6	5

SOURCE: John C. Markowitz, Eva Petkova, Yuval Neria, Page E. Van Meter, Yihong Zhao, Elizabeth Hembree, Karina Lovell, Tatyana Biyanova, and Randall D. Marshall. Is Exposure Necessary? A Randomized Clinical Trial of Interpersonal Psychotherapy for PTSD. *American Journal of Psychiatry*, 2015;172:5, 430–440. Reprinted with permission from *The American Journal of Psychiatry* (Copyright ©2015). American Psychiatric Association. All Rights Reserved.

Table 1.4. CLINICAL CHARACTERISTICS OF PATIENTS WITH PTSD RECEIVING PROLONGED EXPOSURE, IPT, OR RELAXATION THERAPY

Characteristic	Prolonged Exposure (n = 38)		IPT (n = 40)		Relaxation Therapy (n = 32)		Overall Sample (n = 110)	
	Mean	SD	Mean	SD	Mean	SD	Mean	SD
Number of traumas	2.95	1.96	2.63	1.79	2.84	1.67	2.80	1.81
Age at primary trauma (years)	27.7	13.60	24.2	13.7	26.9	15.8	26.2	14.2
	N	%	N	%	N	%	N	%
Trauma type (primary)								
Interpersonal	34	89	37	93	31	97	102	93
Acute	20	53	16	40	10	31	46	42
Chronic	18	47	24	60	22	69	64	58
Sexual abuse	11	29	17	43	11	34	39	35
Physical abuse	25	66	22	55	21	66	68	62
Trauma onset								
Early (before age 13)	6	16	10	25	6	19	22	20
Adolescent (ages 14–20)	4	11	7	18	6	19	17	16
Adult (age 21 or older)	28	74	23	58	18	56	69	63
Missing data	0	0	0	0	2	2	2	2
Previous treatment								
Psychotherapy	27	71	27	68	28	88	82	75
Pharmacotherapy	18	47	19	48	15	47	52	47
Current major depressive disorder	20	53	20	50	15	47	55	50
Recurrent major depressive disorder	12	32	14	35	11	34	37	34
Current generalized anxiety disorder	8	21	3	8	3	9	14	13
Axis II disorders								
Paranoid	6	16	11	28	11	34	28	25
Narcissistic	3	8	7	18	5	16	15	14
Borderline	2	5	2	5	1	6	5	5
Avoidant	7	18	8	20	8	25	23	21
Dependent	2	5	1	3	0	0	3	3
Obsessive-compulsive	10	26	11	28	6	22	27	25
Depressive	6	16	9	23	12	38	27	25
Passive-aggressive	4	11	7	18	5	16	16	15
Any Axis II diagnosis	18	47	17	43	19	59	54	49
Lifetime substance abuse	3	8	5	13	4	13	12	11
Lifetime alcohol abuse	7	18	11	28	4	13	22	20

SOURCE: John C. Markowitz, Eva Petkova, Yuval Neria, Page E. Van Meter, Yihong Zhao, Elizabeth Hembree, Karina Lovell, Tatyana Biyanova, and Randall D. Marshall. Is Exposure Necessary? A Randomized Clinical Trial of Interpersonal Psychotherapy for PTSD. *American Journal of Psychiatry*, 2015;172:5, 430–440. Reprinted with permission from *The American Journal of Psychiatry* (Copyright ©2015). American Psychiatric Association. All Rights Reserved.

Table 1.5. OUTCOMES OVER TIME FOR PATIENTS WITH PTSD RECEIVING PROLONGED EXPOSURE, IPT, OR RELAXATION THERAPY

| | Descriptive Summary | | | | | | | | | | | | |
| | Prolonged Exposure | | | | | IPT | | | | | Relaxation Therapy | | |
Outcome Measure and Assessment Time	N	Mean	SD	Change From Baseline[d]	Effect Size[e]	N	Mean	SD	Change From Baseline[d]	Effect Size[e]	N	Mean	SD
Clinician-Administered PTSD Scale													
Baseline	37	72.1	18.2			40	68.9	16.2			30	68.9	16.4
Week 7	29	39.9	21.0	29.0	1.72	37	50.5	22.3	18.0	1.07	23	54.3	30.8
Week 14	28	37.5	28.8	31.6	1.88	36	39.8	24.3	28.6	1.69	24	46.5	31.0
Posttraumatic Stress Scale–Self-Report													
Baseline	30	77.7	22.3			32	74.3	20.2			23	83.2	15.3
Week 7	19	43.0	23.4	28.6	1.44	31	57.6	24.2	15.2	0.76	17	61.9	28.0
Week 14	17	34.1	26.4	36.1	1.81	23	41.7	26.1	32.1	1.61	13	64.7	27.4
Hamilton Depression Rating Scale (24 items)													
Baseline	33	20.2	6.7			37	18.3	6.5			28	21.0	7.1
Week 7	29	14.0	8.1	5.8	0.86	36	16.3	8.2	2.0	0.30	22	18.2	10.6
Week 14	28	12.3	8.8	7.3	1.07	35	13.8	8.8	4.2	0.62	23	14.8	9.1
Social Adjustment Scale–Self Report													
Baseline	27	2.7	0.6			33	2.7	0.6			21	2.8	0.4
Week 7	20	2.4	0.5	0.3	0.53	34	2.5	0.5	0.2	0.36	16	2.5	0.6
Week 14	15	2.1	0.5	0.4	0.81	22	2.2	0.5	0.5	0.93	14	2.7	0.6
Quality of Life Enjoyment and Satisfaction Scale													
Baseline	31	43.5	14.7			31	43.9	15.0			21	43.1	8.7
Week 7	21	55.8	15.1	−11.8	−0.88	32	51.9	15.1	−8.9	−0.66	17	52.2	20.0
Week 14	15	63.5	19.2	−17.9	−1.33	24	54.6	18.3	−11.3	−0.84	14	46.1	19.2
Inventory of Interpersonal Problems													
Baseline	30	1.7	0.6			32	1.6	0.6			23	1.5	0.4
Week 7	21	1.4	0.4	0.4	0.69	34	1.5	0.7	0.1	0.15	17	1.7	0.7
Week 14	16	1.1	0.6	0.7	1.26	23	1.0	0.7	0.5	0.95	14	1.5	0.6

IPT = Interpersonal Psychotherapy; PE = Prolonged Exposure; RT = Relaxation Therapy.

[a] Generalized linear mixed-effects models (GLMMs) with the imputed data; outcomes at weeks 7 and 14 are modeled as functions of treatment and time, adjusting for baseline value of the outcome and major depression status.

[b] Difference between treatments, p value of the difference, and effect size of the difference.

		Time-by-Treatment Interaction[c]		Difference and Effect Size[b] PE—RT			IPT—RT			IPT—PE		
Change From Baseline[d]	Effect Size[e]	χ²	p	Difference	p	Effect Size	Difference	p	Effect Size	Difference	p	Effect Size
		1.07	0.343									
16.9	1.00											
22.3	1.32			−14.93	0.010	−0.88	−9.47	0.097	−0.56	5.46[f]	0.323	0.32
		4.67	0.010									
20.4	1.02			−16.51	0.053	−0.83	2.20	0.769	0.11	18.71	0.005	0.94
14.1	0.71			−30.75	<0.001	−1.55	−18.22	0.008	−0.92	12.54	0.053	0.63
		0.128	0.880									
4.6	0.68											
7.0	1.03			−4.42	0.034	−0.65	−0.98	0.642	−0.14	3.44	0.065	0.51
		3.875	0.022									
0.1	0.24			−0.15	0.359	−0.26	0.00	0.989	0.00	0.14	0.241	0.26
0.1	0.16			−0.57	<0.001	−1.05	−0.46	0.001	−0.83	0.12	0.409	0.21
		3.561	0.037									
−5.9	−0.44			4.73	0.285	0.35	0.88	0.831	0.07	−3.85	0.302	−0.29
−0.8	−0.06			17.83	<0.001	1.33	10.13	0.017	0.75	−7.69	0.061	−0.57
		3.327	0.029									
−0.1	−0.21			−0.27	0.064	−0.49	−0.13	0.358	−0.23	0.15	0.251	0.26
−0.1	−0.19			−0.58	<0.001	−1.03	−0.53	<0.001	−0.95	0.05	0.771	0.08

[c] Test for interaction between time and treatment from GLMMs for the outcomes at weeks 7 and 14, adjusting for baseline value of the outcome and major depression status. If the interaction term is significant, differences between treatment groups are estimated at each time point; if the interaction term is not significant, a GLMM is fitted without the interaction term, and a single contrast between treatments is estimated, valid for both time points.

[d] Mean change from baseline, based on only the participants with data at week 7 or at week 14.

[e] Effect size of the change from baseline.

[f] The null hypothesis for inferiority of IPT compared with PE (difference of 12.5 points on the Clinician-Administered PTSD Scale) is rejected ($p = 0.035$), thus establishing non-inferiority of IPT.

Dropout is an important treatment outcome. Attrition was 15% in IPT, 29% in Prolonged Exposure, and 34% in the Relaxation Therapy group (n.s.). Two patients from each treatment condition withdrew after randomization but before beginning therapy. Rates of response (defined *a priori* as > 30% improvement in CAPS score) were 63% for IPT, 47% for Prolonged Exposure, and 38% for Relaxation Therapy. IPT had a significantly higher response rate than Relaxation Therapy (χ^2 = 4.45, p = 0.03). Between-group treatment remission rates did not differ significantly: 26% for Prolonged Exposure, 23% for IPT, and 22% for Relaxation Therapy.

On the PSS-SR, patients in the Prolonged Exposure and IPT groups showed statistically significantly greater improvement in PTSD symptoms compared with those in the Relaxation Therapy group (p < 0.001 and p = 0.008, respectively). Patients receiving Prolonged Exposure improved faster than patients receiving IPT and showed an advantage on the PSS-SR over the IPT group at week 14, although this did not reach statistical significance (p = 0.053) (Table 1.5). Prolonged Exposure and IPT each yielded improvement statistically superior to Relaxation Therapy on the Hamilton Depression Rating Scale, the Quality of Life Enjoyment and Satisfaction Scale (Endicott et al., 1993), the Social Adjustment Scale (Weissman & Bothwell, 1976), and the IIP (Horowitz et al., 1988), and they did not differ significantly from each other.

We examined two key associated variables. To ensure that IPT therapists were not conducting unintentional or surreptitious exposure therapy, we conducted mediation analyses that assessed early change (between baseline and week 5) in "frequency of avoidance" of the three highest-ranked trauma items on our Self-Initiated in Vivo Exposure Scale as a predictor of week 14 CAPS score. Early change in frequency of avoidance directly (and expectedly) predicted CAPS outcome for Prolonged Exposure and Relaxation Therapy, but not for IPT (see Figure 1.2). This finding supports Prolonged Exposure and IPT treatment theories.

Half of the patients with chronic PTSD also met criteria for comorbid major depressive disorder, which proved to be a striking moderator of treatment outcome. The study was not powered to detect interaction terms, but in order to avoid omitting potentially important effects due to low power, interactions between treatment and major depressive disorder status with p values ≤ 0.15 were followed up with pairwise comparisons. The omnibus test assessing whether dropout depended on the interaction between depression status and treatment showed a p value of 0.15. Half of patients who had comorbid depression and were assigned to receive Prolonged Exposure dropped out, yielding an odds ratio for Prolonged Exposure attrition with (50%) and without (5.6%) major depression of 17:1 (Table 1.6). Dropout among depressed patients in Prolonged

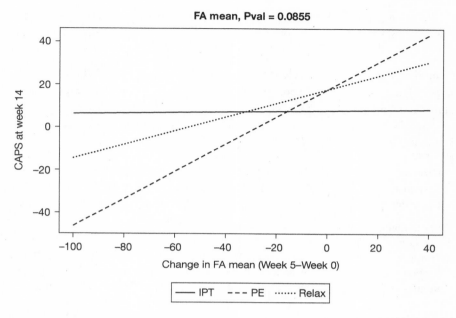

Figure 1.2. Does IPT work through exposure?

Exposure tended to be higher than among depressed patients in IPT ($p = 0.086$) and higher than dropout among nondepressed patients receiving Prolonged Exposure ($p = 0.006$). Dropout among nondepressed patients in Relaxation Therapy tended to be higher than dropout among nondepressed patients in either IPT ($p = 0.068$) or Prolonged Exposure ($p = 0.065$). The effect of the interaction between major depression status and treatment response fell short of statistical significance ($p = 0.058$).

Response rates among patients without major depression were higher for IPT ($p = 0.008$) and Prolonged Exposure ($p = 0.032$) than for Relaxation Therapy. Within the Prolonged Exposure group, response rates were higher among patients without a diagnosis of major depression than among those with depression. No evidence emerged for a moderating effect of depression status on treatment effects with respect to longitudinal PTSD severity (as indicated by CAPS score) or remission status.

Adverse Events. For various reasons, we withdrew five patients from the study. By therapist report and on independent evaluator assessment, two patients in Relaxation Therapy developed worsening depression, one patient in IPT manifested bipolar disorder, one IPT patient engaged in severe recurrent substance abuse, and one Prolonged Exposure patient violated protocol by obtaining outside treatment.

Table 1.6. PROPORTION OF DROPOUT, RESPONSE, AND REMISSION FOR PATIENTS WITH PTSD RECEIVING PROLONGED EXPOSURE, IPT, OR RELAXATION THERAPY, BY COMORBID MAJOR DEPRESSION STATUS

Comorbid Major Depression Status and Outcome	Prolonged Exposure (N = 38)		IPT (N = 40)		Relaxation Therapy (N = 32)	
	N or %	95% CI	N or %	95% CI	N or %	95% CI
With major depression (n = 55):	N = 20		N = 20		N = 15	
Dropout	50	27.2, 72.8	20.0	5.7, 43.7	26.7	7.8, 55.1
Response	30	11.9, 54.3	50.0	27.2, 72.8	46.7	21.3, 73.4
Remission	15	3.2, 37.9	10.0	1.2, 31.7	13.3	1.7, 40.5
Without major depression (n = 55):	N = 18		N = 20		N = 17	
Dropout	5.6	0.1, 27.3	10.0	1.2, 31.7	35.3	14.2, 61.7
Response	66.6	41.0, 86.7	75.0	50.9, 91.3	29.4	10.3, 56.0
Remission	38.9	17.3, 64.3	35.0	15.4, 59.2	29.4	10.3, 56.0

CI = confidence interval

Other Findings. Before randomly assigning patients to treatment, we first explained to them what the three treatments were, using written material and a balanced spoken script. The descriptions emphasized that Prolonged Exposure was much better-studied as a treatment for PTSD than was IPT. After answering patient questions, we asked them whether they had preferences for or would rather not receive any of the study treatments. (They understood that they would not in fact be given a choice amongst them.)

Eighty-seven (79%) patients voiced treatment preferences or disinclinations: 29 (26%) preferred Prolonged Exposure, 29 (26%) preferred Relaxation Therapy, and 56 (50%) preferred IPT (Cochran's Q = 18.46, $p < 0.001$); whereas 29 (26%) were disinclined to Prolonged Exposure, 18 (16%) to Relaxation Therapy, and 3 (3%) to IPT (Cochran's Q = 22.71, $p < 0.001$). (See Figure 1.3.) Overall, treatment preference or disinclination did not predict CAPS change, treatment response, or dropout, but patients who had not only chronic PTSD but also comorbid major depression, and who received unwanted treatment, had worse final CAPS scores.

What this facet of the study showed was that patients were more likely to choose IPT—despite its lack of supporting evidence—than the more grueling exposure-based treatment (Markowitz et al., 2015a). They seemed to prefer focusing on interpersonal issues that were consequences of their traumatic experiences, rather than on the traumatic experiences themselves.

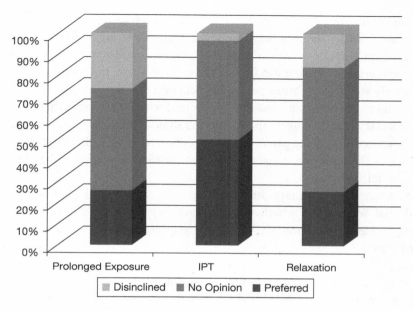

Figure 1.3. Treatment preferences and disinclinations of PTSD patients.
Note: From Markowitz JC, Meehan KB, Petkova E, Zhao Y, Van Meter PE, Neria Y,
Pessin H, Nazia Y: Treatment preferences of psychotherapy patients with chronic
PTSD. *J Clin Psychiatry.* 2015 Jun 9. [Epub ahead of print]: figure 1 on page e4.
Copyright 2015, Physicians Postgraduate Press. Reprinted by permission.

Another study finding concerned personality disorders. Many patients presenting for treatment with chronic PTSD appear to have personality disorders,
although it can be hard to gauge whether, for example, paranoid and avoidant
traits truly reflect personality disorders or represent an overlap with the mistrustful, fearful state of chronic PTSD. Our study evaluated patients before
· and after the 14 weeks of study psychotherapy—psychotherapy that targeted
PTSD, not personality disorders. Expert, reliable raters used the Structured
Clinical Interview for *DSM-IV* Personality Disorders (SCID-II; Gibbon et al.,
1997) for these assessments (Markowitz et al., 2015b).

Forty-seven (47%) of 99 SCID-II patients evaluated at baseline received at
least one SCID-II diagnosis: paranoid (28%), obsessive-compulsive (27%), and
avoidant (23%) personality disorders (PD) were most prevalent. Among 78 patients who repeated SCID-II evaluations post-treatment, 45% (*n* = 35) had baseline PD diagnoses, which 43% (*n* = 15/35) lost at week 14. Three (7%) patients
without baseline PDs acquired diagnoses at week 14; ten others shifted diagnoses. Type of psychotherapy and PTSD response were unrelated to PD improvement. Of treatment responders reevaluated at follow-up (*n* = 44), 56% with any
baseline Axis II diagnosis had none at week 26 (Markowitz et al., 2015b).

This is the first evaluation of the effects of brief Axis I treatment on personality disorder stability. We found that acutely treating a chronic state decreased apparent trait—across most PDs observed, and across the three study psychotherapies. These novel findings have limitations: the study sample was relatively small to measure personality change; few patients had borderline personality disorder, which is often comorbid with PTSD. Nonetheless, these preliminary results suggest that clinicians should not worry too much about the presence of seeming personality disorders in treating patients with chronic PTSD, as the personality disorders may at least in some cases represent artifacts of PTSD itself.

Summary: The primary study goal of this randomized controlled clinical trial was to test whether IPT, a non–exposure-based treatment, was comparable—or no more than minimally inferior—to Prolonged Exposure for patients with severe, chronic PTSD. We indeed found IPT no more than minimally inferior to Prolonged Exposure on the CAPS, the primary outcome measure. IPT had a non–statistically significant but clinically meaningful higher response rate; and it had a lower dropout rate among patients with comorbid major depression. Hence IPT appeared overall roughly equipotent to Prolonged Exposure, the best-studied, gold standard exposure-based treatment for PTSD.

These findings contradict the widespread clinical belief in PTSD therapeutics that patients require exposure to trauma reminders, generally through CBT. This news may be a relief to many patients who refuse to face their trauma-related fears, cannot tolerate systematic exposure, or do not benefit from it. It may also come as a relief to many therapists who seek alternatives to exposure-based treatment (Markowitz et al., 2015). In combination with the previous trials described in this chapter, the results of this study provide reasonably strong empirical support for using IPT as a treatment for chronic PTSD.

Prolonged Exposure took effect more rapidly than IPT, and it showed a slight (non-significant) edge in CAPS score outcome and an advantage just short of significance on the self-report PTSD measure.

Many severely traumatized patients who had reported ineffective community treatment responded within 14 weeks to each of the three study treatment modalities. In a trial that achieved less than planned enrollment, Relaxation Therapy, an active control, statistically differed only marginally from IPT on CAPS score outcomes. A larger sample size might have yielded statistical significance. No ideal psychotherapy control exists comparable to pill placebo in pharmacotherapy trials. A study strength is that Prolonged Exposure and IPT, competing against a robust, active control condition, still showed differential benefits in symptoms and social functioning. This trial potentially adds a novel, very differently focused, non-CBT modality to the PTSD armamentarium.

Two other critical findings arose. First, comorbid major depressive disorder strongly predicted dropout in the Prolonged Exposure group, but not in the IPT or Relaxation Therapy treatment groups. Prolonged Exposure was developed to target anxiety, not depression. Although it does often reduce depressive symptoms (Schneier et al., 2012; Jayawickreme et al., 2014), exposure therapy may be less effective in treating major depressive disorder. Alternatively, it makes clinical sense that comorbid major depression may have rendered tolerating Prolonged Exposure more difficult for patients. Meanwhile, IPT was originally developed to treat major depression, and IPT did so in this study, even while focusing on PTSD. The outcomes suggest differential therapeutics: IPT may have advantages over Prolonged Exposure for patients with comorbid PTSD and major depression.

Few prior studies had even examined PTSD remission rates—none, to our knowledge, had examined remission rates for comorbid PTSD and major depression. The very low remission rates we observed across treatments for patients with PTSD and comorbid major depression (10–15%; Table 1.6) suggest that this group might benefit from combined treatment with both empirically supported psychotherapy and medication (Schneier et al., 2012). Prolonged Exposure may produce greater CAPS score improvement (and have less attrition) in patients without major depression.

A key study mediator suggests that treatment mechanisms differed among the treatments. Unsurprisingly, given the focus on confronting traumatic reminders, patients in Prolonged Exposure who faced their traumas early in treatment had better PTSD outcomes, whereas Prolonged Exposure patients whose avoidance of trauma reminders increased early on had worse final symptom scores than those whose avoidance did not increase early. Such early avoidance had no predictive value in IPT, which deliberately ignores exposure to trauma reminders. IPT may work through alternative, attachment mechanisms involving emotional understanding, social support, and learning to cope with current life (Bleiberg & Markowitz, 2005; Markowitz et al., 2009; Lipsitz & Markowitz, 2013; Markowitz et al., 2014) rather than confronting past traumas. Yet, in order to achieve remission from PTSD, patients must eventually face their fears. As we previously found (Bleiberg & Markowitz, 2005), patients who improved in IPT seemed to gain confidence in daily social interactions, gathered social support, and then spontaneously—without therapist encouragement—exposed themselves to trauma reminders.

We found what many have suspected: exposure therapy is valuable, but not a *sine qua non* for treating patients with PTSD. IPT and CBT both relieve major depression and bulimia. Psychotherapy and psychopharmacotherapy each ameliorate syndromes, presumably via different mechanisms. So why expect only one royal road (Freud, 1913) to PTSD response?

Some of the study findings echo results from other trials. IPT, which initially focused on affective attunement and only later in treatment encouraged PTSD patients to change their interpersonal interactions in current relationships, yielded somewhat slower symptom improvement than Prolonged Exposure, but caught up over time. This pattern resembles some eating disorder comparative trials, in which IPT therapists, barred from discussing binge eating and body image in bulimia, focused entirely on interpersonal relationships. In those studies, IPT yielded slower improvement than CBT but eventually pulled even (Weissman, Markowitz, & Klerman, 2000). The IPT approach to affective attunement also evokes Cloitre and colleagues' PTSD treatment study (2010), in which initial affective attunement and social skills training (based on dialectical behavioral therapy principles, rather than IPT) preceding exposure therapy benefited patients more than exposure therapy alone.

Researcher allegiance can influence study outcomes (Luborsky et al., 1999; Falkenström et al., 2013). I, the study's principal investigator, had clear links to IPT, hence it is possible that some patients entered the study seeking IPT. This seems unlikely, however, given their evident lack of psychotherapeutic knowledge at study entry and our PTSD clinic's historical specialization in Prolonged Exposure treatment (Schneier et al., 2012). We encouraged a friendly rivalry among the three psychotherapy teams, which were all supervised by experts in the respective approaches and monitored for therapist adherence. In a previous trial at our Columbia/New York State Psychiatric Institute treatment site, in a trial clearly allegiant to Prolonged Exposure (Schneier et al., 2012), the same Prolonged Exposure therapists achieved comparable results: a 45% response rate, compared with 44%, using identical criteria (Schneier, personal communication, Oct. 2013); and a 29% dropout rate, compared with 28%. Our study findings of Prolonged Exposure superiority over Relaxation Therapy confirm assay sensitivity.

No research is perfect. Strengths of this study included matched rival teams of dedicated, allegiant psychotherapists. Few previous PTSD trials have defined response or remission *a priori*. The proscription of pharmacotherapy in the treatment sample eliminated the confounding effects of undocumented pharmacotherapy dosage changes and of potential psychotherapy–pharmacotherapy interactions. On the other hand, proscribing pharmacotherapy very probably contributed to the study's limited sample size by excluding patients who were receiving psychopharmacotherapy. We felt it would have been inappropriate to stop antidepressant medications for prospective study patients that, even if ineffective for PTSD, might benefit depressive or anxiety symptoms. A larger sample would have had increased statistical power to test between-treatment differences. The unmedicated status of this patient sample may also limit the generalizability of our findings. A further limitation is our failure to complete two session adherence ratings on every treatment dyad, although all of those we rated were adherent.

The hypothesized *a priori* margin of 12.5 CAPS points to define "not more than minimal inferiority" between Prolonged Exposure and IPT derived from a literature review (Weathers et al., 2001) and statistical estimation based on our pilot data (Bleiberg & Markowitz, 2005). Our empirical CAPS data suggest a much narrower (5.5-point) clinical difference between the two treatments. Our smaller-than-intended sample size had the effect on testing this hypothesis of increasing the probability of type II statistical error: that is, of not rejecting the null hypothesis when it is false. Here it means that there was a greater than 20% chance of failing to reject the null hypothesis of IPT's having been more than minimally inferior to Prolonged Exposure when in fact IPT was not more than minimally inferior. The smaller sample size may also account for our failing to find differences between IPT or Prolonged Exposure versus Relaxation Therapy on some outcome variables. Finally, although even the planned sample size did not allow sufficient power to detect clinically meaningful treatment-effect moderators, the smaller-than-intended sample size further reduced its power for moderation hypotheses.

The findings of this comparative trial require replication in combat veterans (only two of our 110 participants were veterans), in other PTSD populations, and at other treatment centers with differing treatment allegiances. Treatment mechanisms require further exploration. In any case, having another potentially efficacious treatment will benefit patients with PTSD (Markowitz et al., 2015).

SUMMARY OF THE EVIDENCE

The best-studied treatments for PTSD are exposure-based versions of Cognitive Behavioral Therapy: Prolonged Exposure, Cognitive Processing Therapy, EMDR, and the like. This reflects the larger picture of CBT domination of anxiety disorder research (Markowitz et al., 2014). CBT thinking even influences DSM symptom criteria for diagnoses like PTSD. IPT, a newer entry to the field of anxiety disorders, may nonetheless provide an alternative, well tolerated approach to treating chronic PTSD.

CBT is a diverse treatment. The term actually encompasses several treatments, varying in their emphases on cognitive or behavioral interventions. As a result, therapists expert in panic-centered treatment (i.e., CBT for panic disorder) may have little familiarity with CBT for depression or Prolonged Exposure for PTSD. In contrast, IPT has—for better or worse—remained recognizably similar across disorders, despite adaptation for particular cultural and psychopathological issues inherent in each treatment population. Hence, if you already know IPT for depression (still the modal target for IPT) and have had some experience in treating patients with PTSD, it should take relatively little adjustment to apply IPT to PTSD.

After our research came out, someone introduced me at a conference as "the guy who disses CBT." This has never been my intent. I am a card-carrying member and Founding Fellow of the Academy of Cognitive Therapy. I trained at Aaron Beck's cognitive therapy program in Philadelphia. I treat patients with CBT in my private practice and have supervised therapists in CBT. I believe CBT works, and our study confirmed previous trials of Prolonged Exposure in demonstrating it did so. So I don't disrespect CBT; I just don't think it's the only way to do psychotherapy with patients. The history of psychotherapy describes all too many fractures and guild wars, when in fact psychotherapists of all stripes should be working together to ensure that patients get the best, empirically validated treatments. For patients who don't want, or who haven't responded to, an exposure-based treatment, it's good to have an alternative like IPT.

2

The Target Diagnosis

PTSD

One of the things which danger does to you after a time is—well, to kill emotion. I don't think I shall ever feel anything again except fear. None of us can hate any more—or love.
—GRAHAM GREENE, *The Confidential Agent. New York: Penguin, 1980, page 18*

WHAT IS PTSD?

PTSD, the target diagnosis for IPT in this book, is a prevalent, debilitating syndrome. Rates of PTSD in the general population range run to 3.5% annually (Kessler, Chiu et al., 2005) and 6.8% over a lifetime (Kessler, Berglund, et al., 2005). Among soldiers returning from the recent wars in the Middle East, PTSD has reached epidemic proportions, with some 14% meeting diagnostic criteria (Wisco et al., 2014; Hoge et al., 2014; Wisco et al., in press).

Developing PTSD, like any medical disorder, involves some interaction of biological vulnerability and environmental insult. Different people carry different risks, as do different environmental traumas. As we've discussed, the diagnosis of PTSD requires a severe trauma (pages 3–4) that is associated with a variety of anxious, dissociative, arousal, and re-experiencing symptoms. This is a diagnosis that upends your life, diminishing functioning and ruining relationships.

Although decades of research have characterized aspects of PTSD, these studies have also made evident the heterogeneity of PTSD. It matters when in your life the trauma hits you, and for how long. Which of the following traumas seems worse?

Repeated physical and sexual abuse in childhood
or
Involvement in a fatal motor vehicle accident at age 45?

In the case of later-onset trauma, a person's personality has had a chance to form, and hopefully, the person has achieved a stable sense of the world and of relationships. The trauma of a car accident is awful, particularly if your wife dies in the seat beside you. Yet a therapist might hope that if such a person presents for treatment of PTSD, the patient will have the resources of having developed an untraumatized personality and sense of self; a history of stable relationships; potential social supports (even if, in suffering from PTSD, the patient has withdrawn from supportive relationships); and a relatively brief period of trauma (albeit with a lengthy aftermath).

By contrast, a person who grows up knowing nothing besides abuse faces multiple difficulties: an interpersonal style affected by trauma from the very start; less of a sense of stable relationships, because interpersonal relationships have been tinged and traumatic from the beginning; fewer available social supports; and the damaging experience of repeated trauma over an extended period of time. Trauma that begins before your personality has had a chance to form, before your world has acquired any sense of stability, affecting your childhood and adolescent development, must be worse than a single, later-onset trauma. This has been something of a clinical consensus for years, with some writers distinguishing between "simple" and "complex" PTSD.

Which sounds worse to endure:

A devastating hurricane, earthquake, or tsunami
or
Rape?

Impersonal traumas like natural disasters can constitute *DSM-5* Criterion A traumas for PTSD, but in general, interpersonal traumas are worse. The idea that someone has done something to hurt you—that malice, cruelty, or depraved indifference plays a role—ratchets up the severity of the experience (Norris et al., 2002). Janoff-Bulman (1992) called this "human-induced victimization."

Yet all of these sorts of trauma can produce PTSD. Furthermore, patients with all of these traumatic events appear treatable: despite the sense that compound, prolonged trauma is worse, it has been difficult to demonstrate that the type of trauma affects the treatment outcome. Still, it's important from a clinical perspective to consider what sort of trauma the patient has, what that trauma means to the patient, and what the consequences of that trauma are: the particular sensory and psychological triggers that may provoke symptoms.

There are many other ways to divide the diagnosis. Military cases of PTSD appear harder to treat (although again, they are not untreatable), perhaps because of both the severity of the traumatic experience and the difficulty veterans face in readapting and re-assimilating to civilian society upon their return from the front. *DSM-5* distinguishes between subtypes of PTSD: a preschool classification, for children less than six years old; and a dissociative subtype, for patients who feel detached and depersonalized, and with delayed expression (Table 2.1).

Making the Diagnosis of PTSD. Clinicians generally make the diagnosis of PTSD based on the *DSM-5* criteria. The first key issue concerns whether the patient has experienced a trauma (*DSM-5* Criterion A) sufficient to qualify for the diagnosis. This has been a problem in the past: the severity threshold for the trauma needed to make the diagnosis has fluctuated among DSM editions, as well as in the hands of different therapists. The original diagnostic criterion, established in the DSM-III in 1980, was that the trauma needed to be extraordinarily upsetting, a life-threatening catastrophe: "a recognizable stressor that would evoke significant symptoms of distress in almost everyone" (American Psychiatric Association, 1980, p. 238). This followed the historical connection of PTSD with combat trauma, "shell shock," and "battle fatigue," along with the growing recognition that American soldiers had suffered great traumas in the Vietnam war. Subsequent DSM revisions loosened the definition of trauma. This raised problems, however.

First, to define the severity of the traumatic event by the patient's subjective perception rather than objective measures threatens to render the idea of a traumatic event meaningless: everyone has his or her own definition of upsetting events. Almost everyone will experience a (rigorously defined) *DSM-5* Criterion A traumatic event over the course of a lifetime, yet only a relatively small fraction of individuals develop PTSD (Kessler et al., 1995; Breslau et al., 1998). Yet if trauma becomes a loosely defined matter of what one feels is "traumatic," then trauma becomes ubiquitous, and uninformative.

What constitute "merely" terrible events, but not *DSM-5* "trauma"? This inevitably becomes an arbitrary distinction. For example, the death of a close family member is painful and sad, but also sometimes expectable: a 97-year-old grandmother who dies in her sleep; a favorite dog who dies at age 14. Therefore, *DSM-5* attempts to distinguish between the death of a loved one and the *traumatic* death of someone, and similar qualifications. (See Table 2.1, criterion A.3.; and A.4 note.)

Second, some individuals will present for treatment with anxiety symptoms, avoidance, recurrent nightmares, negative cognitions, and physiological

Table 2.1. DSM-5 SYMPTOM CRITERIA FOR PTSD

A. Exposure to actual or threatened death, serious injury, or sexual violence in one (or more) of the following ways:
  1. Directly experiencing the traumatic event(s).
  2. Witnessing, in person, the event(s) as it occurred to others.
  3. Learning that the traumatic event(s) occurred to a close family member or close friend. In cases of actual or threatened death of family member or friend, the event(s) must have been violent or accidental.
  4. Experiencing repeated or extreme exposure to aversive details of the traumatic event(s) (e.g., first responders collecting human remains; police officers repeatedly exposed to details of child abuse).
  Note: Criterion A4 does not apply to exposure through electronic media, television, movies, or pictures, unless this exposure is work-related.
B. Presence of one (or more) of the following intrusion symptoms associated with the traumatic event(s), beginning after the traumatic event(s) occurred:
  1. Recurrent, involuntary, and intrusive distressing memories of the traumatic event(s).
  Note: In children older than 6 years, repetitive play may occur in which themes or aspects of the traumatic event(s) are expressed.
  2. Recurrent distressing dreams in which the content and/or affect of the dream are related to the traumatic event(s).
  Note: In children, there may be frightening dreams without recognizable content.
  3. Dissociative reactions (e.g., flashbacks) in which the individual feels or acts as if the traumatic event(s) were recurring. (Such reactions may occur on a continuum, with the most extreme expression being a complete loss of awareness of present surroundings.)
  Note: In children, trauma-specific reenactment may occur in play.
  4. Intense or prolonged psychological distress at exposure to internal or external cues that symbolize or resemble an aspect of the traumatic event(s).
  5. Marked psychological reactions to internal or external cues that symbolize or resemble an aspect of the traumatic event(s).
C. Persistent avoidance of stimuli associated with the traumatic event(s), beginning after the traumatic event(s) occurred, as evidenced by one or both of the following:
  1. Avoidance of or efforts to avoid distressing memories, thoughts, or feelings about or closely associated with the traumatic event(s).
  2. Avoidance of or efforts to avoid external reminders (people, places, conversations, activities, objects, situations) that arouse distressing memories, thoughts, or feelings about or closely associated with the traumatic event(s).
D. Negative alterations in cognitions and mood associated with the traumatic event(s), beginning or worsening after the traumatic event(s) occurred, as evidenced by two (or more) of the following:
  1. Inability to remember an important aspect of the traumatic event(s) (typically due to dissociative amnesia and not to other factors such as head injury, alcohol, or drugs).
  2. Persistent and exaggerated negative beliefs or expectations about oneself, others, or the world (e.g., "I am bad," "No one can be trusted," "The world is completely dangerous," "My whole nervous system is permanently ruined").

Table 2.1. CONTINUED

3. Persistent, distorted cognitions about the cause or consequences of the traumatic event(s) that lead the individual to blame himself/herself or others.
4. Persistent negative emotion state (e.g., fear, horror, anger, guilt, or shame).
5. Markedly diminished interest or participation in significant activities.
6. Feelings of detachment or estrangement from others.
7. Persistent inability to experience positive emotions (e.g., inability to experience happiness, satisfaction, or loving feelings).
E. Marked alterations in arousal and reactivity associated with the traumatic event(s), beginning or worsening after the traumatic event(s) occurred, as evidenced by two (or more) of the following:
1. Irritable behavior and angry outbursts (with little or no provocation) typically expressed as verbal or physical aggression toward people or objects.
2. Reckless or self-destructive behavior.
3. Hypervigilance.
4. Exaggerated startle response.
5. Problems with concentration.
6. Sleep disturbance (e.g., difficulty falling or staying asleep or restless sleep).
F. Duration of the disturbance (Criteria B, C, D, and E) is more than one month.
G. The disturbance causes clinically significant distress or impairment in social, occupational, or other important areas of functioning.
H. The disturbance is not attributable to the physiological effects of a substance (e.g., medication, alcohol) or another medical condition.

Specify whether:
With dissociative symptoms: The individual's symptoms meet the criteria for posttraumatic stress disorder, and in addition, in response to the stressor, the individual experiences persistent or recurrent symptoms of either of the following:
1. Depersonalization: Persistent or recurrent experiences of feeling detached from, and as if one were an outside observer of, one's mental processes or body (e.g., feeling as though one were in a dream; feeling a sense of unreality of self or body or of time moving slowly).
2. Derealization: Persistent or recurrent experiences of unreality of surroundings (e.g., the world around the individual is experienced as unreal, dreamlike, distant, or distorted).
   Note: To use this subtype, the dissociative symptoms must not be attributable to the physiological effects of a substance (e.g., blackouts, behavior during alcohol intoxication) or another medical condition (e.g., complex partial seizures).

Specify whether:
With delayed expression: If the full diagnostic criteria are not met until at least six months after the event (although the onset and expression of some symptoms may be immediate).

arousal symptoms (for example, panic attacks), thus meeting *DSM-5* Criteria B through D for PTSD. Yet if these patients report qualifying symptoms but no plausible trauma, they should be treated for a different diagnosis, not for PTSD.

Differential diagnosis of PTSD requires deciding whether the patient better qualifies for an adjustment disorder, acute stress disorder (duration: three days to one month), or other trauma- or stressor-related disorder. In addition, the diagnosis of PTSD should be contextualized by psychiatric and medical co-morbidity. Major depressive disorder is a particular concern, as it presents in roughly half of patients diagnosed with PTSD (Shalev et al., 1998). Other anxiety disorders, substance use disorders, personality disorders, and phys-ical trauma (that is, traumatic brain injury [TBI]; Stein et al., 2015) also may inform clinical decision making.

Our study, which began in 2008, used the then-current *DSM-IV* (1994) criteria for PTSD. These have been altered somewhat for *DSM-5*, which ar-rived in 2013 (see Table 2.1), although the two sets of diagnostic criteria appear roughly comparable (Hoge et al., 2014). Research trials do not simply rely upon DSM criteria, but also typically measure the severity of PTSD symptoms using rating instruments. I strongly recommend this procedure, even for clinicians in non-research settings. Assessing PTSD severity at the start of treatment helps to clarify the diagnosis. Furthermore, it provides initial psychoeduca-tion for patients who may have difficulty in distinguishing between who they are and the disorder they have. Thus, using a clinical rating instrument helps patients recognize PTSD symptoms as such and begin to regard them as sepa-rable from themselves, and ego-dystonic.

Nor should rating end with diagnosis. Serial assessment, another regular feature of outcome research studies, involves repeating the rating scale at reg-ular intervals over the course of treatment. For a 14-week treatment like IPT, the therapist might want to administer the scale, not only at the start of treat-ment, but at week 4, week 8, week 12, and after completing week 14. Or at least at weeks 7 and 14. Repeating the measure reinforces patients' understanding of the symptoms of PTSD. Beyond that, it keeps both therapist and patient at-tuned to progress (or lack thereof) in the treatment. Patients may not always recognize how much they are improving. A score on an established PTSD scale may help them do so and encourage them to proceed.

For screening purposes or as a patient self-report instrument, clinicians might want to use a measure such as the PTSD Checklist (PCL-5; Weathers et al., 2013). This is a 20-item scale, with each item rated 0–4. It takes just a few minutes to complete; a score of 38 appears to demarcate clinical severity. Clinicians can obtain the measure at no cost from the scale available from the National Center for PTSD at www.ptsd.va.gov.

The best-established observer-rated instrument for PTSD is probably the Clinician-Administered PTSD Scale (CAPS; Blake et al., 1995; Weathers et al., 2001; Weathers et al., 2013a). The 30-item CAPS-5, released in 2013, asks the rater to assess the 20 *DSM-5* symptom criteria for PTSD (Table 2.1, criteria B–E), gauging their frequency and intensity on a scale of 0 (absent) to 4 (extreme/ incapacitating) (Weathers et al., 2013a). It can take almost an hour to administer, but this may be worth it, as the CAPS-5 delves into the type of trauma and the nature of symptoms in detail. Like reviewing the *DSM-5* criteria with a patient, this may help reify the diagnosis as something the patient may not always have had, and in any case as a disorder, something distinct from the patient as a human being.

The PCL-5 and CAPS-5 each have different versions for the interval of recent symptoms (e.g., past week, versus past month, versus worst month). Numerous alternative PTSD scales exist. Which scale you use in treating patients may matter less than that you use one. Because patients with PTSD suffer from numbness, emotional detachment, and alexithymia, as well as mistrust of others (including therapists), some may initially under-report symptoms, then "wake up" in the course of treatment to an increased recognition of their (hopefully receding) suffering.

Serial rating of patients over the course of a time-limited therapy has always been a feature of IPT, which arose in a research setting where such assessment was standard conduct (Markowitz & Weissman, 2012). An initial evaluation should of course include more than a PTSD measure: a history of present illness, psychiatric and family psychiatric histories, medical and social history, and mental status examination (American Psychiatric Association, 2015).

Treatment Planning. Once having made the diagnosis, the clinician should present it to the patient. *Giving the patient a diagnosis, and explaining that it is a treatable condition, and not the patient's fault,* is a standard maneuver of IPT therapists. It deserves to be used in any treatment plan. It helps patients know what afflicts them, and that it is treatable. Moreover, many patients suffer from guilt and self-blame as symptoms of their syndrome: this is true for both major depression and PTSD. Abused children, for example, frequently hear from their parents or other abusers that everything is their fault, and believe against all reason that their persecutors must be right. Combat soldiers frequently feel responsible for the witnessed death of a comrade ("survivor guilt"), even though the death was in no way their doing (Aakvaag et al., 2014). Hence, explaining the disorder and exculpating the patient frequently get treatment off to a good start.

The next question is the crucial matter of differential therapeutics: which treatment is likely to help the patient most? Several time-limited psychotherapies and several pharmacotherapies for PTSD have been empirically validated.

Or treatments: what about combining medication and psychotherapy (Schneier et al., 2012)? I suggest that therapists not be dogmatic. Many or most therapists have a preferred treatment, which they employ most frequently and with which they feel most comfortable. Treatment, however, is supposed to follow informed consent, and informed consent should include a balanced discussion of empirically proven available options, addressing their pros, cons, and empirical support. It helps patients to know that multiple treatment options exist, and that if one treatment does not help, another well may. Patient treatment preference tends to matter (Markowitz et al., 2015a), and showing the patient that you value and respect the patient's input is likely to enhance the therapeutic alliance (Cloitre et al., 2002, 2004), again starting treatment on a positive note. This may have particular value in working with patients suffering from PTSD, who mistrust their environments and the people in them. Different treatments may also have particular advantages for particular patients, based on studies of moderating variables, such a comorbid depression (see Chapter 1).

Offering the patient a time-limited rather than an open-ended psychotherapy has several advantages. First, it is the time-limited psychotherapies that have received empirical validation (in part because their brevity makes research funding feasible). Thus you can tell the patient that there is evidence backing the treatment approach. Second, if the treatment does not help the patient, it has a reasonably brief course and a definable end, after which the patient can move on to an alternative treatment (Markowitz & Milrod, 2015). Not to define an end to treatment risks years of unhelpful if well-intended therapy.

Third, and perhaps most important, many patients who have PTSD may have lived with its symptoms for decades, if not their whole lives. They often take years to reach treatment: a median delay of 12 years, according to one study (Wang et al., 2005). If, when they do present for treatment, a therapist can offer them a proven (albeit not guaranteed) treatment that may relieve many of their symptoms in a matter of weeks, that paradoxical gambit of time-limited treatment for a chronic condition may provide a therapeutic shock. Patients may think or say, "You mean I don't have to live like this?" They may remain skeptical about the treatment until they are better, but the idea that a condition that has lingered for years can be treated acutely carries therapeutic weight (Markowitz, 1998).

Readers of this book will most likely practice psychotherapy (or hopefully, psychotherapies) and, like most patients with mood and anxiety disorders, you may prefer psychotherapy to medication as a treatment (McHugh et al., 2013). Nonetheless, the medication option should not be ignored. Pharmacotherapy rarely induces remission in PTSD, but it can help greatly (Marshall et al., 2001).

As Schneier et al. showed in a small study, the serotonin reuptake inhibitor (SRI) paroxetine (Paxil) augmented the effects of Prolonged Exposure therapy, with combined treatment yielding better effects than Prolonged Exposure alone (Schneier et al., 2012). I tend to find sertraline (Zoloft) better tolerated, and there is a research literature showing that it, like paroxetine, reduces PTSD symptoms. Whatever gets the patient better is the ultimate means to the ultimate end of recovery.

3

A Pocket Guide to IPT

Man is a social animal.

—BARUCH SPINOZA

BACKGROUND

Several manuals illustrate the use of interpersonal therapy (IPT) as a treatment for major depression (Klerman et al., 1984) as well as for other psychiatric disorders (Weissman et al., 2000; Weissman et al., 2007). For lack of space, this book cannot accommodate the detail of those manuals in its focus on PTSD. Instead, this chapter outlines the basic principles of IPT as a time-limited, diagnosis-targeted treatment for psychiatric disorders. It thus necessarily compresses a complex treatment—IPT is not the most complicated of psychotherapies, but no psychotherapy is simple. (Readers may want to consult the standard IPT manuals [Klerman et al., 1984; Weissman et al., 2000; Weissman et al., 2007] for greater detail.) Chapter 4 of this book, describing the adaptations of IPT for treating patients with chronic PTSD, incorporates the basic IPT principles listed here.

Interpersonal Psychotherapy, developed in the 1970s by Myrna Weissman, the late Gerald L. Klerman, and their colleagues at Yale and Harvard universities, was initially intended as a treatment for major depressive disorder (Klerman et al., 1984; Markowitz & Weissman, 2012). IPT not only acutely relieved depressive symptoms better than a control condition and comparably to medication, but on follow-up, IPT improved interpersonal functioning, which medication alone did not (Weissman et al., 1976). Combined treatment with IPT and medication proved better in treating major depression than either alone (DiMascio et al., 1979). A series of randomized controlled clinical trials has since repeatedly demonstrated its efficacy, not only for that disorder, but for unipolar depression in various treatment populations, for eating disorders (Weissman et al., 2000), as an adjunctive treatment for bipolar disorder (Frank et al., 2005), and to a lesser degree, for some anxiety (Markowitz et al., 2014) and other disorders. Researchers have sequentially adapted IPT for different diagnoses, cultural populations of patients, and treatment formats. In general, these adaptations have been detailed in treatment manuals tailoring the basic IPT treatment to the particular clinical circumstance. This book expands upon the treatment manual we used in our NIMH-funded research trial (Markowitz et al., 2015).

IPT is based on theories of attachment and interpersonal functioning derived from Harry Stack Sullivan (1953), John Bowlby (1969), and others (Klerman et al., 1984; Markowitz et al., 2009; Lipsitz & Markowitz, 2013). The IPT approach emphasizes human beings as social animals and links patients' feelings to their interpersonal context. IPT balances interpersonal theory with practical, pragmatic, clinically informed interventions. When Gerald L. Klerman, Myrna M. Weissman, and their colleagues were developing the treatment in the 1970s, they built it upon empirical data about interpersonal interactions and the relationship of mood disorders to life events (Markowitz & Weissman, 2012).

BASIC PRINCIPLES

Klerman and Weissman knew that depressed individuals withdrew from social interaction, spoke less, did less, and functioned less well than others (Klerman et al., 1984). Depressed individuals become passive, resigned, helpless, and hopeless. Klerman and Weissman also knew that interpersonal events frequently triggered depressive episodes. Based on these theories and data, Klerman, Weissman, and colleagues developed a time-limited, diagnosis (namely, major depression)–targeted treatment that used these core principles:

1. Depression is a medical illness
2. Life events affect mood, and *vice versa*

Depression Is a Medical Illness. Defining depression as a *medical* illness was a radical idea in the 1970s; it has hopefully become mainstream now. Talcott Parsons (1951) and others had described the social role of the medical patient: that having an illness was a socially accepted role, with privileges (being excused from work you cannot do when ill) and responsibilities (to be a good patient, work at getting better). Studies had shown that depression was as or more debilitating than many other medical diagnoses (Stewart et al., 1989). Klerman and Weissman therefore medicalized depression as *a debilitating but treatable problem that is not the patient's fault* (Klerman et al., 1984).

If depression is an illness, it follows that patients should not be blamed for their condition—most especially by themselves—but should blame the depression itself (as they might an infection, or asthma), and work towards regaining health. If nowadays major depression is much more accepted as an illness than regarded as a failing or weakness as it was in the 1970s, the idea of shifting blame and guilt from the guilty patient to the mood disorder—recognizing guilt as a depressive symptom—nevertheless remains a very helpful maneuver with guilty, self-critical patients. IPT therapists generally try to support the patient, tending to shift blame either to depressive symptoms or to the oppressive environment that the patient needs to address.

Life Events Affect Mood, and Vice Versa. Following a stress-diathesis model, the IPT outlook recognizes that mood disorders do not occur in a vacuum, but rather in an interpersonal context. Upsetting events trigger upset moods, and bad moods tend to trigger even more bad events. Thus a severe life event may trigger a depressive episode in an individual vulnerable to depression. Once the person develops depressive symptoms, life tends to go badly: the individual sleeps poorly, awakens tired and disorganized, is concentrating poorly, can't find her keys on leaving the house; misses the train; arrives at work late, and there has negative interactions with co-workers. These negative events compound the already depressed mood, contributing to a sense of helplessness, hopelessness, and futility. This in turn worsens her functioning, in a continuing negative spiral (see Figure 3.1).

IPT uses an understanding of this pattern to treat depression, working on both a "macro" and a "micro" level. The bigger picture is to help the patient link the onset or worsening of depressive symptoms to a life event. This link

Figure 3.1. Moods and events interact.

can be approached in either direction: that is, the event may trigger the depressive episode, or a depressive episode may trigger negative life events. The direction does not matter as much as the connection: the therapist wants the patient to understand that events affect mood, and *vice versa*.

There are four interpersonal problem areas, all based on empirical psychosocial evidence about depression, that IPT uses to focus treatment. Each represents a life crisis: the death of a significant other (*grief*, or *complicated bereavement*), a struggle in a relationship with a significant other (a *role dispute*), or a major life change such as starting or ending a job, starting or ending a relationship, receiving the diagnosis of a serious illness, etc. (a *role transition*). In the absence of these life events, a misleadingly named residual category has been (unfortunately) titled *interpersonal deficits*. This is better understood as an absence of life events, a debilitating situation of often-chronic social isolation (Weissman et al., 2007).

After taking a careful history in the early sessions (generally sessions 1–3 in a 12–16-session weekly treatment; fewer than three sessions if possible), the therapist asks the patient if the therapist can present a formulation (Markowitz and Swartz, 2007).

"You've given me a lot of helpful information. Can I ask you whether I understand your situation?"

The therapist then summarizes the patient's history of present illness, establishing that the patient is suffering from a major depressive episode and linking this episode to a life event.

"As we've discussed, you have all the symptoms of major depression, and you scored a 25 on the Hamilton Depression Scale, which indicates your depression is pretty severe. It may feel hopeless—that's one of the symptoms of depression—but it's a treatable condition, and you have a good chance of getting better. From what you've told me, your symptoms seem to have begun after your daughter died, an overwhelmingly upsetting situation that we call 'complicated bereavement.' It seems to have brought your life nearly to a halt. What I would suggest is that we spend the remaining nine weeks of treatment focusing on what this terrible loss means for you, how to handle the painful feelings it brings up, and how you can begin to move on with your life. Does that make sense to you?"

Usually it does make a lot of sense, the patient agrees to the formulation, and it thereafter becomes the focus of treatment. So on a broad, structural level, the linkage of mood (disorder) and life events becomes the focus of IPT treatment. The formulation makes this explicit in a helpful, organizing way for bewildered and overwhelmed patients (Markowitz & Swartz, 2007; Weissman et al., 2007).

Although it is possible that the patient's story will yield several plausible formulations, you will only want to choose one problem areas as a focus (or, in rare cases, two). Part of the organizing effect of the formulation should be to simplify the patient's complex story into a manageable package: Something bad happened, you've been traumatized, and now let's look at what PTSD is doing to your interpersonal life. In general, you will want to choose the focus that seems most emotionally salient.

On a "micro" level, the therapist connects mood and events in each treatment session. Every session after the first one begins with the question:

"How have things been since we last met?"

This elicits one of two answers: either a mood ("I've been feeling terrible"; "I've been so depressed") or an event ("It was my birthday"; "I was fired from my job"; "I had another fight with my wife"). If the patient responds with a mood, the therapist replies:

"I'm sorry to hear that. Did something happen that worsened your mood?"

If the patient has presented an event, the complementary question is:

"How did that make you feel?"

Thus after two questions, the IPT therapist has pinpointed a recent, affectively charged life event, which represents an ideal target for psychotherapy. If, as is usually the case early in treatment, the mood and event are both negative, the therapist sympathizes, then tries to reconstruct the event with the patient to understand why and where things went wrong.

"What did you say? ... What did he say? ... Then how did you feel? ... Then what did you say?"

This sequence helps determine fluctuations in the patient's mood, dissonance between what the patient felt and what the patient said, and a sense of the patient's interpersonal style in an encounter. Following this reconstruction, the therapist helps the patient recognize maladaptive interpersonal patterns, often shifting undue blame from the patient to the weight of depressive symptoms or to the other party in the encounter. ("It's hard to confront other people when you're feeling so depressed.") Therapist and patient then explore alternative options for handling such situations, and subsequently role-play them so that the patient can build comfort and familiarity with self-assertion, confrontation, and other non-depressed interpersonal maneuvers (Weissman et al., 2007).

This is the heart of IPT. Some of the principles inherent in this approach are:

- Mood disorders have an interpersonal context, and can be treated through improving the interpersonal environment.
- Resolving an interpersonal crisis should improve not only your life circumstances but also your mood.
- Even in the midst of an overwhelming personal crisis, when one is feeling passive, helpless, and hopeless, one can take charge of one's life and improve one's situation.
- *IPT builds social skills.* It should be evident why: the therapy focuses almost entirely on recognition of affects in interpersonal situations; validation of those affects; and helping the patient use the feelings, often by verbalizing them, to improve interpersonal situations.

These principles have been borne out by multiple randomized clinical trials, the gold standard in clinical outcome research.

Other important aspects of IPT include:

- *Mobilizing social support.* The perception that you are not alone, but have people you can count on and turn to, makes a huge difference in preventing or relieving a range of psychopathologies, including major depression and PTSD (Markowitz et al., 2009). Being able to talk to someone about one's fears and concerns, rather than keeping them in as a terrible secret, and receiving validation or support in return, is a great relief. Thus a goal of IPT is to help patients to identify, bolster, and use social supports. To do this, the therapist conducts an *interpersonal inventory* (Weissman et al., 2007) during the initial, history-taking sessions of IPT, to develop a sense not only of how the patient relates to others, but of who those others are. Does the patient have potential allies, even if depression or anxiety or PTSD mistrust is inhibiting the patient from engaging with them? Who, conversely, may be causing trouble in the patient's environment (perhaps causing a role dispute that might be the focus of treatment)? The members of the interpersonal inventory often come into play in the treatment that follows.

- *Setting a time limit.* Time pressure can work wonders. Although not all disorders lend themselves to a time-limited approach, mood and anxiety disorders certainly do. Telling a patient that he or she will end treatment in a matter of weeks, probably feeling better, has several therapeutic benefits. For patients who feel hopeless, it presents a constructive paradox: How can my therapist really think I'll get better so fast, when I strongly doubt I'll get better at all? Beyond that, the time frame pressures both patient and therapist into action. This is a powerful prod for depressed and anxious patients who feel passive, helpless, and hopeless.
- *Deciding whether or not to prescribe medication.* Because of its medical model, IPT is nicely compatible with pharmacotherapy. Just as a patient with diabetes might receive both a behavioral intervention (psychoeducation, diet, exercise, regular glucose testing, etc.) and insulin, a patient with major depressive disorder may benefit from both IPT and antidepressant medication. Not all psychotherapies have such theoretical compatibility with medication.

THERAPEUTIC STANCE

The IPT therapist's stance is encouraging, supportive, hopeful. This does not mean projecting sugary sweetness, which can lead a patient to feel misunderstood and trivialize the patient's suffering (Markowitz & Milrod, 2011). Rather, the therapist acknowledges the patient's suffering, helps the patient sit with and tolerate rather than avoid painful affects, then helps the patient recognize the utility of feelings like anger, sadness, and anxiety. The patient is in pain, but there is hope for interpersonal gains and symptomatic recovery. The initial message is: You're in pain . . . but there is hope.

The IPT therapist tries to function as a helpful coach, an expert in treating the target disorder. The therapist encourages the patient to see his or her own strengths, even if symptoms threaten to obscure them. Rather than feeding the patient suggestions, the therapist asks, "What options do you have?" and, if need be: "What you have tried before?" The therapist shifts undue blame for situations from the patient to the depressive disorder, or to the interpersonal environment, rather than siding with the patient's depressive self-criticism. The patient gets credit for accomplishments that occur during the treatment: the therapist can make apparent that it is the patient who has tested out a new interpersonal approach or made a life change, and that this active work by the patient has produced therapeutic gains.

IPT therapists apologize if they make mistakes or if the patient feels hurt by an interchange. They do not generally self-disclose, but neither do they attempt a neutral, impassive stance: they try to model decent interpersonal behavior.

PHASES OF IPT

Acute treatment is divided into three logical phases.

Phase 1. In the *initial phase*, generally sessions 1–3 out of 12, the therapist introduces him- or herself to the patient and begins to take a history. This generally includes using a rating scale to measure the target diagnosis: for example, the Hamilton Depression Rating Scale (Hamilton, 1960). In taking a history, the therapist focuses on interpersonal issues. Goals include:

- Getting a sense of who the patient is, how he or she functions, in an interpersonal context. How does the patient generally interact with others? Is the patient overly trusting, or mistrustful? How does he or she handle anger? (Many depressed and anxious patients suppress it as a "bad" feeling rather than expressing it.) Are there maladaptive (depressive) patterns in relationships?

- Taking an *interpersonal inventory* of relationships, close and distant, starting with childhood but focusing on the present, where relationships can still be addressed. Who are the important people in the patient's life? Who are actual or potential social supports? Who may contributing to the patient's difficulties?

- If the patient has been in previous therapies, it is worth exploring how he or she felt in them. Did the patient ever object to anything a therapist said? If so, did the patient just think it, or say so? IPT therapists do not work in the transference, and the focus of IPT is generally outside rather than inside the office. Nonetheless, IPT therapists recognize the therapeutic alliance as crucial, and acknowledge the therapeutic relationship as a situation about which the patient can have and voice feelings. An IPT therapist might offer: "If anything makes you uncomfortable here, please bring it up. I'm not trying to bother you, and that's just the sort of issue that it might be worth discussing" (Markowitz et al., 2007).

- Setting the time limit. IPT for depression is generally set at 12 (or 8, or 16—but it's important to choose a number and stick to it) weekly sessions. It's not actually clear what an optimal psychotherapy "dosage" is—pharmacotherapy studies routinely have investigated dosage, but few psychotherapy studies have. The key point is to create a time frame to create an urgency to move the therapy forward.

- Giving the patient the medical model: depression is a treatable illness.
- Providing the formulation.
- Other logistics: generally scheduling sessions once a week, with contingencies for emergencies, anticipation of vacations, etc.

Phase 2. Once the patient agrees with the formulation the therapist has presented—and this is almost always the case—IPT enters its *middle phase* (sessions 4–9). This focuses on treatment of the interpersonal focus that the formulation has established. Beginning with the opening gambit ("How have things been since we last met?"), the therapist uses specific strategies to explore the patient's feelings in interpersonal situations. The strategies differ somewhat for *complicated grief, role dispute, role transitions,* and *interpersonal deficits,* but the basic issues are the same: How do you feel? What does that feeling (or those mixed feelings—it's possible to have more than one) tell you about your interpersonal situation? Is it reasonable that you should feel that way, given the situation? And if it is reasonable to feel sad/angry/anxious, what can you do with that feeling? What options do you have? Then role-play feasible options to gain comfort in actually using the feelings. Again, this frequently involves asserting one's wishes or dislikes to other people.

In *complicated grief (complicated bereavement),* a significant other has died and the patient has become depressed. The goal is to help the patient grieve and begin to move on. Goals of treating complicated grief include:

- *Tolerating the affect.* Many patients in this situation have been afraid to grieve, feeling that the affect would be overwhelming and destructive. "If I started to cry, I would never stop. I'd crumble." IPT therapists try to normalize affect, allowing catharsis and processing of the emotions. Therapist ask about why the lost person and relationship were important: "What do you miss about—? . . . What do you miss about the relationship you had?" Over time, it is also helpful to explore mixed feelings, even though (or more precisely, *because*) many depressed patients feel awful that they might dislike or even hate someone who is dead. "What didn't you like? . . . Every relationship has frictions, difficulties. . . . It's possible to love and hate someone at the same time."

- *Regaining a direction.* Many patients struggling with complicated grief find themselves adrift; stuck, empty. They may have stopped working at their jobs to care for an ill relative, then find themselves without a job as well as without the relationship. As patients start to express their feelings and feel better, it's important to help them find other social supports to replace the lost relationship, as well as a new purpose and direction in life. Sometimes this relates to the death of the other: for example, volunteering for the American Diabetes Association.

Patients presenting with a *role dispute* are invariably losing a battle in a relationship. The concept of a role dispute is that both members of a relationship have needs, likes and dislikes, and they hopefully compromise on these to their mutual satisfaction. Depressed and anxious patients tend to avoid confrontation, to see anger as a "bad" feeling, and so tend to submit to the demands of others without presenting their own needs and wishes. The goal of treating a role dispute is to help the patient (1) recognize that disparities in a key relationship are contributing to the depressive episode, and (2) learn to renegotiate the relationship to a more equitable and satisfying equilibrium.

Patients in a *role transition* find themselves in the midst of a life change that feels overwhelming. This could be a change in a relationship (marriage, divorce), a job change, a geographical move, the birth of a child, the diagnosis of a serious illness, or any other disturbing life event. This has clear application to PTSD, a disorder defined by a life event. Treating a role transition resembles treating complicated grief, although here no one has died. The framework of a "role transition" helps the patient recognize the connection between the life change and mood change; the therapist encourages the patient by affirming that, as he or she accommodates to the change, things should settle down.

Because, as with grief, patients tend to see the past as having been stable and happier, and the present as miserable and hopeless, the therapist explores how the patient feels about the loss of the old role ("What was good about being married?") while encouraging mourning for what has been lost. At the same time, the therapist helps the patient see limitations of the past role and weigh both negative and positive aspects of the new role. Even difficult new roles generally have some positive aspects.

The IPT focal problem area of last resort, *"interpersonal deficits"* means that the patient's history lacks the central life event on which IPT usually focuses. No one has died; there is no role dispute or role transition. Instead, the therapist must focus on the patient's social isolation, which is often chronic, and point out that this isolation or social difficulty is contributing to their depressed mood. The goal is to cautiously build social skills so that the patient can gain social comfort in interpersonal interactions and social supports in his or her environment.

Phase 3. The final few sessions of acute treatment constitute the *termination phase*. Its multiple goals include consolidating the patient's gains during treatment, dealing with the separation of ending, and looking ahead to the future. If the patient has improved, the IPT therapist asks, "Why are you feeling better?" The answer generally leads to the understanding that the patient has improved because of his or her own efforts. Patients tend to credit their therapists for improvement, but it's important to give patients who have been feeling helpless and passive a sense of their own agency and independence, particularly when they are leaving treatment. The structure of IPT generally makes it clear that the therapist may have functioned as a helpful coach, but that the patient has done the hard work: having quelled a role dispute, for example. This is an opportunity to identify and reinforce interpersonal skills the patient has developed during the treatment.

If the patient remains symptomatic but IPT has clearly reduced symptoms, it may be appropriate to conclude acute treatment but to make a new treatment contract for continuation of IPT. Similarly, if the patient has remitted but faces a high risk of relapse, maintenance IPT—perhaps at a lesser frequency, such as once fortnightly or once a month—has been shown to have a protective effect (Frank et al., 1990; Frank et al., 2007). If the patient has not significantly improved, termination becomes an opportunity to review whatever gains the patient has made—often the patient has achieved some interpersonal progress, but symptoms have not responded—and to emphasize that the therapy, not the patient, has failed. This medical model echoes a pharmacotherapy trial: if one treatment doesn't work, that's disappointing, but thankfully there are alternative treatments available. The crucial issue is that the patient not blame him- or herself and feel too discouraged to continue in another, potentially more helpful treatment (Markowitz & Milrod, 2015).

Separation generally evokes sadness, but the patient may have various feelings about stopping therapy, including anxiety about having to function on his or her own, relief at no longer having to attend sessions, etc. The IPT approach does not focus on transference, but rather on the patient's emotional responses to ending what has hopefully been a helpful relationship.

Termination is also a moment to anticipate issues in the patient's future. What aspects of the interpersonal focus remain unresolved, and how might the patient want to address them? What problems are likely to arise over time?

4
—

Adapting IPT for PTSD

A difference, to be a difference, must make a difference.
—GERTRUDE STEIN

This manual adapted Interpersonal Psychotherapy for use by therapists in a 14-week treatment study of chronic posttraumatic stress disorder. It is intended as a guideline for treatment, as an extension of the basic IPT manual (Weissman et al., 2007), and as an adjunct to IPT supervision. *Although IPT for PTSD does involve some adaptations from standard IPT for major depressive disorder, if you have previously used IPT, the basic approach is the same and should feel familiar to you.* This was certainly the experience of therapists in our randomized trial (Markowitz et al., 2015), who had previously treated major depression. When they began the study in 2008, we told the therapists that an open trial of IPT for PTSD had yielded very encouraging results (Bleiberg & Markowitz, 2005), as had a randomized trial of group IPT for PTSD (Krupnick et al., 2008).

A key issue in the 2015 randomized trial was to ensure that IPT therapists not conduct an exposure-based treatment. That is, IPT could not involve encouraging patients to face and habituate to fearful reminders of traumatic events. IPT is not inherently exposure-based, but we wanted it to be clear that no exposure was taking place. IPT supervision and adherence ratings of IPT tapes helped guarantee the purity of psychotherapeutic approaches. Indeed, for IPT we added an adherence item, asking raters to judge (see Figure 4.1).

Exposure therapies (exemplified by Prolonged Exposure) and IPT start from the same premise that the patient has experienced a traumatic event—trauma being the necessary precursor to the diagnosis of PTSD. But whereas exposure-based therapies then focus on reconstructing jumbled memories of the trauma, creating a hierarchy of feared trauma reminders, and sequentially exposing the

To what degree did the therapist encourage the patient to expose him/herself to feared trauma reminders?

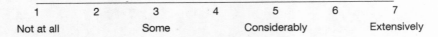

1	2	3	4	5	6	7
Not at all		Some		Considerably		Extensively

Figure 4.1. Non-exposure adherence item.

patient to these until he or she habituates to the stimulus and stops feeling so frightened, IPT takes a very different approach. Table 4.1 summarizes some differences between IPT for PTSD and exposure-based treatments for PTSD.

The elements of IPT remain unchanged: there is an initial, a middle, and a termination phase. The therapist provides the patient with a medical model: *PTSD is a debilitating but treatable disorder that is not the patient's fault.* The treatment focus remains on emotions and interpersonal circumstances. We adapted IPT to a degree, however, to address the specific issues that patients with chronic PTSD face.

1. *Affective reattunement.* One clinical difference between patients who present with major depression and those with chronic PTSD is that

Table 4.1. DIFFERENCES BETWEEN EXPOSURE THERAPIES
AND IPT

	Exposure-Based Treatment	IPT
Focus	Traumatic events Narrative of trauma Reminders of trauma	Current interpersonal relationships
Treatment principle	Exposure to trauma reminders; Habituation diminishes fear	Interpersonal emotions; attachment, support
Goal	Reconstructing trauma history, habituation to trauma reminders	Improving and restoring emotional life and interpersonal functioning
Temporal focus	Largely on the time of the trauma(s), focusing on what happened	The present, focusing on interpersonal sequelae of having been traumatized
Discussion of trauma	Extensive, throughout	Minimal, at outset
Message to patient	Face your fears, and they will go away	Your emotions can help you manage your relationships and decide whom you can trust; some people can provide helpful support
Homework	Yes, daily	None

the former can easily tell you how they're feeling, whereas the latter often report being numb, almost alexithymic (Markowitz et al., 2009). It is therefore crucial to help these patients (re)gain a connection with their emotions. Simply helping patients tolerate emotions that they perceive as dangerous represents a therapeutic gain. To further encourage patients to see that these seemingly dangerous feelings can guide social behavior adds another dimension to patients' interpersonal skills and functioning. Thus we devote much of the early weeks of IPT for PTSD—sometimes as much as the first half of the 14-week treatment—to developing a working emotional vocabulary: What kind of "upset" does the patient feel? What do you call that feeling? Is that a reasonable response to the situation? What does it tell you about the situation? A goal of IPT for PTSD is to give patients comfort with the feelings they are desperately avoiding, particularly negative affects like anger, sadness, and anxiety; and a chance to reflect on what they mean.

Thus although IPT is time-limited, and that time limit pressures the patient to move ahead in treatment and in life, toleration of affect is not a domain to rush through. As a therapist, you want to demonstrate and to have the patient experience that **emotions, although powerful, are not dangerous.** You can accomplish this task by pausing and silently and attentively sitting with the patient while he or she feels something and has a few moments to reflect upon it, survive it, and hopefully to recognize its pertinence to an interpersonal situation. Although you, too, may feel uncomfortable if the patient seems very angry or very sad, your job is to sit with it, encourage it; to show poise, and to show that you're not afraid of the emotion. Changing the subject or rushing ahead conveys an avoidance of emotion that is precisely what you do not want to show. This is an important difference between an affect-focused therapy and some other treatment approaches.

Once the patient is in touch with his or her feelings, and the therapist has helped the patient normalize them, the next step is to utilize those feelings, often by verbalizing them, in addressing interpersonal encounters.

For many patients presenting with chronic PTSD, it is difficult to know whether they once had greater awareness of their feelings and then lost this after they developed PTSD and became numb. Alternatively, they may always have been relatively alexithymic—able to manage life without awareness of their feelings—until the weight of emotional response overwhelmed this adjustment. The first circumstance may be easier to address, as it simply requires bringing a patient back to awareness rather than teaching an emotional understanding and vocabulary from scratch. From an IPT perspective, however, exactly how the patient became so out of touch with his or her feelings does not really matter. The critical points are that the patient is emotionally detached and numb, that PTSD has either caused or exacerbated this, and that understanding one's feelings is essential in order to be able to decode interpersonal interactions, to determine who in one's environment is potentially trustworthy and a social support, and who is not.

2. *Focus on the interpersonal aftereffects of trauma.* Exposure therapies focus on reconstructing the trauma the patient has experienced, and therefore on the past. IPT, however, acknowledges that the patient has experienced a severe trauma but (perhaps surprisingly) makes no attempt to reconstruct the traumatic event(s). In the initial session, the therapist briefly asks about what happened to the patient: "What was the trauma that provoked PTSD?" But having established that a trauma occurred, the focus is not on building a coherent narrative of the event, eliciting and helping the patient habituate to upsetting moments. The goal is simply to establish the trauma as antecedent to, and explanation for, PTSD symptoms. Indeed, the trauma receives no further mention as such.

Instead, the IPT therapist focuses on the present, and on the *interpersonal consequences of the trauma rather than the trauma itself.* What effect has the trauma had on the patient's social relationships, use of social supports, and trust of other people? What havoc has the trauma wreaked on current relationships, and where is the patient having difficulty in dealing with other people as a consequence of PTSD? Patients who do not want to relive their traumatic incidents do not have to; many have expressed relief on this account (Markowitz et al., 2015a).

Patients in IPT are told that they have PTSD, an anxiety disorder linked to the terrible trauma they have experienced. The therapist points out that this is not the patient's fault, and that unfortunately many people are traumatized. IPT-PTSD then focuses on the interpersonal sequelae of PTSD. *People who develop PTSD suffer from interpersonal problems.* Among the key consequences of PTSD are:

a. Affective detachment—emotional distancing from people and daily life
b. Mistrust of the environment—particularly when the trauma has been an interpersonal one, inflicted by someone else; and
c. Interpersonal hypervigilance.

The patient withdraws from activities (*DSM-5* PTSD symptom C.2), feels estranged from others (symptom D.6), experiences a constricted affect (symptom D.7), often with outbursts of irritability (symptom E.1), and not only a physiological but an interpersonal hypervigilance (symptom E.3) and mistrust (symptom D.2) (American Psychiatric Association, 2013). Note that whereas exposure-based treatments tend to address PTSD B and C criterion phenomena, IPT focuses on the more interpersonal items. The DSM emphasis on cognitive and behavioral symptoms to define PTSD may to some degree reflect the dominance of Cognitive Behavioral Therapy (CBT) as a treatment for the disorder. Interpersonal aspects may to some degree have been underplayed.

The IPT therapist takes the position that it's unfortunate enough that the patient has suffered the precipitating trauma; the patient needn't be doubly punished or cheated by losing his or her social life and sense of place in the world as well. That's literally "*adding insult to injury*." Treatment therefore represents a reparative *role transition* from a traumatized to a healthy state, in which the patient reclaims his or her former level of functioning. (This is the concept of an *iatrogenic role transition*, in which the IPT therapist frames the therapy itself as a brief period of recovery from a chronic psychiatric disorder [Markowitz, 1998; Lipsitz et al., 1999].) This role transition can be a particularly germane focus if the patient's traumatic symptoms are longstanding and related to a temporally distant trauma, analogous to patients treated with dysthymic disorder and social phobia in other IPT studies.

Again: although the therapist must acknowledge the patient's trauma as a serious and naturally upsetting event, and must review the trauma during the initial history-taking, the *subsequent focus of treatment is not on the traumatic event, but on its reverberations in numbed emotions, shattered social relationships, and loss of formerly pleasurable activities and routines.*

How IPT works is unknown. It is plausible that PTSD symptoms improve in IPT because IPT-PTSD encourages patients to tolerate affect, to risk potentially emotional encounters with others, and to build social supports. IPT helps patients identify their emotions as interpersonal signals and use them to respond appropriately. This leads to interpersonal "success experiences" (Frank, 1971), reassuring patients of environmental mastery. Indeed, symptomatic improvements in PTSD patients from our pilot study correlated with the extent to which patients succeeded in making interpersonal changes in their focal problem area (e.g., role transition) (Markowitz et al., 2006). We surmise from clinical experience that improved mastery in these everyday experiences, together with more secure, "safer" interpersonal attachments, encourages patients to risk confronting traumatic reminders. This is captured scientifically as a reduction in avoidance symptoms. The IPT medical model also normalizes trauma reactions for patients, much as the psychoeducational phase of CBT normalizes symptoms, helping reduce feelings of shame. Even if the mechanism of IPT ultimately proved linked to *in vivo* exposure, yet managed to retain and successfully treat exposure-averse patients, it would finesse an important clinical problem. For patients reluctant to confront traumatic reminders, an interpersonal model could be an effective alternative for engaging them in treatment.

Our modification of IPT for PTSD thus focuses on *how trauma has compromised patients' current interpersonal perspective and social functioning*. We postulate that *trauma impairs the individual's ability to use the social environment to process environmental trauma*. Trauma shatters the individual's sense of environmental safety and poisons his or her trust in interpersonal relationships. Hence the individual with PTSD withdraws from, or distances him- or herself within, relationships, and restricts social activities. This withdrawal prevents the individual from obtaining needed social support. Experiencing the environment and relationships as "dangerous" triggers maladaptive social functioning that helps perpetuate PTSD, whose symptoms in turn reinforce social detachment and dysfunction. IPT may counter the internal perception of helplessness, shame, and interpersonal danger in PTSD with perceived interpersonal understanding and social competence.

The focus of IPT on current relationships shifts the patient's attention from inner preoccupation with past trauma to coping with the immediate interpersonal outer world. Treatment addresses not potentially frightening re-exposure to traumatic memories or reminders, but quotidian encounters with friends, family, and coworkers. By helping patients test their interpersonal environments and recognize that they are safer than their traumatic expectations allow, this approach may help PTSD patients mobilize social supports (Brewin et al., 2000, Ozer et al., 2003) and restore interpersonal functioning, yielding improved interpersonal comfort and generalized symptomatic relief. Mobilizing and increasing available social supports provides a task for the patient while meeting an important clinical need. PTSD patients have withdrawn from available social supports, compounding their isolation and feelings of mistrust. Re-engaging with social supports, or finding new ones, may relieve PTSD symptoms, reintegrate the patient into the social environment, and build interpersonal skills to improve social function.

The process of symptom improvement obviously includes reversal of avoidance patterns, and may to a degree resemble the trajectory of exposure-based therapies. Although IPT-PTSD and exposure therapy for PTSD differ in structure and technique, their primary difference is in therapeutic focus: interpersonal problems vs. behavioral avoidance. Yet for IPT-PTSD to have efficacy, it must ultimately reverse behavioral avoidance despite eschewing elaborate, systematic in vivo hierarchies as primary treatment emphasis.

3. *Mobilizing social supports.* IPT therapists always look for potential social supports in their patients' environments and encourage patients to find and use them. This may have particular salience for benumbed, socially withdrawn patients with PTSD (Brewin et al., 2000, Ozer et al., 2003, Markowitz et al., 2009).

PTSD and Attachment. Underlying the IPT approach is the Bowlbyian concept of *secure attachment* (Bowlby, 1969). Individuals who in childhood find that their parents encourage them to explore the environment and provide reassurance when they do so tend to grow up with secure attachment: they trust their relationships and the people in them. In consequence, they tend to develop larger and more secure social networks than less securely attached people. Should a trauma occur, the securely attached individual will have people to turn to for solace and understanding, and will feel relatively comfortable in doing so. This may allow the securely attached individual to process trauma without developing PTSD. In contrast, individuals who grow up without supportive parenting tend to develop insecure or disorganized forms of attachment (Bowlby, 1969; Fonagy et al., 2002), and hence feel less comfortable in relationships. Should trauma occur, they will have fewer confidants to approach and less confidence in approaching them. With fewer social supports and less social confidence, they are surely at higher risk for PTSD and less likely to be able to use social supports to relieve PTSD symptoms. A consequence of such social isolation and attachment insecurity is that patients keep their painful feelings in, rather than processing them.

Thus a goal of IPT in treating patients with chronic PTSD is to help them use the social supports that may help relieve their symptoms. *It's good not to be alone in a crisis*, to feel you have family or friends who can understand your situation and support your getting through it. By helping patients to understand how they feel in interpersonal situations, and allowing patients to use that understanding to decide whom they can trust, IPT may work to help patients (re)build security of attachment, thereby relieving symptoms.

It is for this reason that we have considered *reflective function* (Rudden et al., 2009), a measure that is a sort of proxy of attachment, a potentially important research tool for understanding change in IPT for PTSD. Reflective function is a psychoanalytic measure of an individual's awareness of his or her own emotions and those of significant others. This measure (Rutimann and Meehan, 2012) thus focuses on an interpersonal target that may be both a target of IPT therapy and a major difficulty for emotionally distanced patients with PTSD.

One would expect reflective function to be very low in patients with PTSD, and that at least aspects of it would improve with successful treatment. In particular, we are conducting research on *symptom-specific reflective function*, the patient's emotional understanding of the PTSD syndrome itself (Rudden et al., 2009).

4. *Choice of Interpersonal Focus.* IPT for mood disorders seems to work better for patients who have life events than for those who do not: namely, the patients whose problems can be categorized as *complicated bereavement, role dispute,* or *role transition,* rather than the no-life-event category known as *interpersonal deficits.* The IPT macro/micro strategy of focusing on feelings and life events may work best conceptually when there is a "macro" defining event (e.g., a trauma) as an interpersonal focus to parallel the "micro" quotidian events that weekly IPT treatment reviews. An advantage of treating PTSD is that all patients will necessarily have a life event, as PTSD by definition requires one. This eliminates the need to use the problematic interpersonal deficits category. For many patients, the focus of PTSD treatment will be a role transition, although clearly the interpersonal disturbance of trauma can cause role disputes, and the complicated grief following the traumatic death of a loved one can trigger PTSD as well. There is an appealing intuitive fit between IPT, a life-events-based treatment, and PTSD, a life-event-based disorder.

Disposing of the interpersonal deficits focus may be a relief to many IPT therapists who know from experience that it's better to have a life event to focus on. Some might wonder, though, what to do with a patient whose early-life child abuse has left them chronically socially isolated, with what appear to be, loosely speaking, "interpersonal deficits." The point of the current approach is that social difficulties are an expected consequence of trauma, and a person abused during childhood has developed PTSD from that trauma, including its interpersonal sequelae. Thus the trauma provides a theoretical fulcrum for understanding current emotional and interpersonal difficulties, which can be treated under the rubric of a role dispute (if the patient still has contact with the abuser) or role transition (if not).

This chapter hopefully makes it clear that, although we have tweaked the treatment slightly, it remains fundamentally the same IPT approach applicable to major depression and other disorders. Such adaptation is appropriate in adjusting a treatment for any new treatment population (cf. Markowitz, 1998; Markowitz et al., 2009a). Thus, for example, emphasizing affective attunement seemed a crucial recalibration for patients with chronic PTSD but is usually far less necessary for depressed patients. This chapter should also clarify that, although IPT in effect "exposes" patients to tolerance of their own emotions, it does not engage in the systematic exposure-based approach of most treatments for PTSD.

5

IPT for PTSD—Initial Phase

Interpersonal therapy for posttraumatic stress disorder generally follows the application of IPT to major depression, with the following modest modifications. IPT is divided into three phases: beginning, middle, and end. Readers may want to refer to the *Clinician's Quick Guide to Interpersonal Psychotherapy* (Weissman et al., 2007) for elaboration on themes discussed here.

The initial phase generally encompasses sessions 1–3 out of 14 total acute-phase sessions. This first phase sets the stage for the remainder of treatment. It has several goals:

1. *Diagnosis,* of both:
   a. *PTSD, as the target diagnosis,* and any comorbidity; and
   b. *the interpersonal context* in which the patient lives with this disorder.
2. *Setting the framework for treatment*
3. *Initial symptomatic relief*

Although it may take as long as three sessions to complete this phase, the goal is to complete it as soon as possible. Depending upon your efficiency as a therapist and the patient's efficiency as an historian, it may sometimes be possible to complete the tasks of this phase sooner and to progress to the crucial middle phase. In any event, you do not want this organizing phase to extend longer than three sessions, because you and the patient need to work on the issues that will help resolve the patient's life crisis and PTSD symptoms.

PHASE 1: DIAGNOSIS

Although in our research studies the patients had already been diagnosed by independent evaluators to ensure that they met study eligibility requirements, the therapist nonetheless reviewed PTSD symptoms (see Chapter 2) and the patient's interpersonal history (Chapter 3). Again, you should use a PTSD rating instrument like the CAPS (Weathers et al., 2013a) or PCL (Weathers et al., 2013) to establish the diagnosis and symptomatic severity of PTSD.

Having diagnosed PTSD, *use a medical model to label PTSD as a treatable illness that is not the patient's fault.* This begins psychoeducation about PTSD. You will also take an *interpersonal inventory* (Weissman et al., 2007) of the social supports, problematic relationships, and patterns of relationships in the patient's life, beginning in the past but concentrating on the present. For IPT-PTSD, this history will include a careful trauma history, looking for patterns of mistreatment, inability to effectively assert oneself or effectively express anger, difficulties with intimacy, anger dysregulation, etc. In taking the interpersonal inventory of the patient's past and present relationships, assess the patient's capacity for intimacy in relationships, capability for self-assertion and confrontation with others, and social risk-taking. If such functioning has clearly become impaired with the development of PTSD, that is worth underscoring. In taking a history, the therapist also assesses current dangerousness (suicidal risk, potential for relapse into substance abuse). The goal will then be to link the two diagnoses—PTSD and its interpersonal context—in the IPT formulation that concludes this opening treatment phase.

Aspects of the early phase include:

A. *Taking a history of present illness, which will inevitably touch on the patient's traumatic event.* Your role as IPT therapist is to make it clear to the patient that, although you need to know what happened to the patient, this is the *only* time it is likely to come up in detail; the therapy will not consist of reconstructing and reliving it. Aspects of the trauma include the patient's brief version of what happened: where he or she was, how risky he or she had thought the situation would be, how long it lasted, how the patient responded during the crisis, feelings the patient had at the time about the event; also when symptoms began, and which ones particularly bother the patient. Are there physical as well as psychic consequences to the trauma: traumatic brain injury (Stein et al., 2015) or other medical debility? You will also eventually want to ask about past traumas: Is this a patient who has repeatedly experienced overwhelmingly frightening events or brutalizations? Depending upon your treatment setting, some of this material may be available from the patient's admission packet, but it is important to at least touch on this with the patient so that you have a shared understanding of what the patient has lived through.

Given the focus of IPT, you will also want to ask about how others around the patient reacted to the traumatic event and what support, if any, they provided. In this context, it is important to ask how much of the story the patient has related to others, seeking support; and how much the patient has kept to him- or herself.

If a patient willingly discusses his or her traumatic history in a session, you can let the patient do so, but you should always bring the focus back to the effect this trauma may have had on their trusting or relating to other people. If the patient is uncomfortable discussing the trauma, acknowledge this as part of the PTSD syndrome and state that it is not necessary to review the trauma in detail. Still, you can continue, it would be helpful to have some general understanding of how other people may have hurt or upset the patient in order to appreciate how traumatic events and consequent PTSD symptoms may have affected the patient's relationship to other people and social situations.

B. *Taking an interpersonal history*: the *interpersonal inventory*. In the same way that you want to understand the patient's relationship to trauma, you also need to know how the patient interacts with other people. You can start with the present or the past, but cover both, and particularly get a sense of recent and current relationships. Who are the important people in the patient's life? In whom can he or she confide feelings, disappointments and upsets? (It's worth mentioning to the patient that having confidants provides protection against symptoms.) How have relationships changed in the wake of the traumatic event?

Further, what patterns have existed in relationships in the past? How close has the individual ever been able to get to other people? How secure is the patient in attachments to others? Has he or she been able to express feelings directly to other people, including love, anger, and his or her needs? How do relationships start and end? What was the family situation like growing up? Friends? Dating?

The goals of the interpersonal inventory include:

- *Finding potential social supports* whom the patient can mobilize even if he or she has not been using them. Whom is the patient closest to? How close? Social supports protect against symptoms and aid recovery. Research has found that being able to tell someone how you're feeling and to share "dark secrets" may be crucial to the outcome of PTSD.
- *Finding potential role disputes*. Are there people in the patient's life who are contributing to interpersonal conflict? Are there relationships

that the patient is having trouble negotiating? These could be a potential focus of the treatment.

- *Getting an overall sense of the patient's interpersonal functioning.* Many patients with PTSD may have had difficulty in forming secure attachments in relationships even prior to the trauma they have suffered. Difficulty in forming such attachments may reflect earlier life traumas or difficult relationships, and may make it hard to mobilize social supports when needed after a recent trauma. Although the focus of IPT is on the present, it's helpful to have a sense of the person's background, starting with childhood and stretching to the present.

The interpersonal inventory is not a formal scale but a collection and weighting of key relationships and patterns of relationships in the patient's life, particularly the patient's current life.

C. The interpersonal inventory and general history of present illness should yield the *focal problem area* on which treatment will center. This could be *complicated bereavement* (if the trauma is associated with violent death or murder), a *role dispute* (if the patient is engaged in a struggle with a significant other, such as an abusive spouse), or a *role transition* (having suffered a trauma and living with its consequences).

D. It will also be helpful to know something about *prior treatment* the patient has received: what the patient has found helpful or unhelpful, and what his or her feelings are about psychotherapy and about medication. If the patient has been in lengthy but unhelpful psychotherapy in the past, you can listen, ascertain what the patient found unhelpful, sympathize, and then explain that IPT is a different, brief, focused kind of treatment for medical problems like PTSD. Your job is to communicate therapeutic optimism and hope. Again, it's good to invite dissent: if the patient doesn't like something that's occurring in the therapy, you welcome the patient's bringing it up: such self-assertion is indeed a goal of the treatment. A past treatment relationship with an abusive therapist obviously requires careful discussion and the explicit setting of appropriate boundaries in the current treatment (see Chapter 11).

E. Having completed these tasks, you offer the patient a *formulation* (Markowitz and Swartz, 2007) that links the diagnosis to the patient's life situation. You might begin this by first complimenting the patient on his or her help in gathering the data you are about to summarize:

"You have given me a lot of information so far. I think I understand what has happened to you, but can I ask you if I've gotten it right?"

Then, for example, you could say:

"You have PTSD, an illness that developed in response to the terrible attack(s) you suffered. Horrible events like yours can really change your outlook and your life: if you experience something painful enough, anyone can develop PTSD. But it's not your fault, and it's a treatable disorder." [Here you might describe some of the PTSD symptoms the patient has recounted.]

"As a consequence of PTSD, you now seem to have trouble trusting all sorts of relationships and situations you face. We call this change the trauma causes a *role transition*. Your life has felt out of control since then. If you can learn to understand PTSD and the transition you're going through—a transition that requires dealing with the interpersonal consequences of your trauma—you can do something about it. *We'll focus on how past trauma is interfering with your current interactions with other people.* I suggest that we work on how you can use your emotional responses to situations to handle this during the remaining 12 weeks of treatment. Your feelings can help you decide who's trustworthy and who isn't. If you can get things under control, your PTSD symptoms may well improve, too. Does that make sense to you?"

Or: "You have PTSD, a treatable illness.... Your continuing distress seems to have something important to do with the *role dispute* you're having with your family, whom you've felt alienated from and who also seem to have been treating you differently since you were raped. I suggest that we work on seeing how you can solve this situation with your family over the remaining 12 weeks of treatment. If you can resolve this dispute, you will probably feel a lot better; and your PTSD symptoms may well improve too. Does that make sense to you?"

Or: "Witnessing the death of your child and feeling you couldn't do anything to prevent it was a horrible event. It's one of the worst life events, the kind of trauma no parent should have to endure, and it's not surprising that you've had trouble getting over it. As a consequence of this extreme trauma, you've developed PTSD. You've been feeling numb, and worry about how you feel, and you've tried to keep it to yourself, but things have been getting worse and worse.

"So your PTSD is connected to this terrible event. We call what you're going through *complicated grief,* and it's taken over your life. I suggest that we spend the remaining 11 weeks of treatment helping you come to terms with your feelings, and figuring out how to proceed in this excruciating situation. Does that make sense to you?"

This formulation defines a focus for the remainder of the treatment. *The patient must explicitly agree* with the therapist on this formulation. Once the patient does, the therapist may steer him or her to that focus from session to session. The formulation works in both directions: PTSD symptoms inhibit social functioning, which in turn reinforces PTSD avoidant symptoms and sense of social distrust.

If a patient were to disagree with your formulation, you could negotiate a different focus. It's important that you recognize the patient's input—good that the patient asserts herself!—and that you and the patient reach an agreement on the goal of therapy. In practice, however, it's extremely rare for patients to disagree with a formulation. IPT interpersonal problem areas generally make sense to patients (Markowitz et al., 2007). Life events, particularly traumatic ones, are undeniable. No patient in either of our PTSD studies ever disagreed with the focus.

PHASE 2: SETTING THE FRAMEWORK FOR TREATMENT

A second aspect of the initial phase is to explain the format of IPT to the patient. Keep in mind that patients with PTSD come to treatment feeling overwhelmed, assaulted, and out of control. They fear unpleasant surprises around every corner; they never know what's coming next, but they anticipate that it will be bad. Under these circumstances, your job is to make the office a safe place, to preclude as many surprises as possible.

You can do this in several ways. Just taking a professional stance, eliciting a history, diagnosing the disorder, and linking it to the patient's interpersonal context in the formulation should emanate a sense that you've dealt with PTSD before, know how to treat it, and know that it's treatable. If you are calm, caring, attentive, respectful, and understanding (using the "common factors"—see the end of this chapter), that will help, too. By structuring the framework of treatment for the patient, letting him or her know what to expect, you can further defuse fears about what will happen in treatment and communicate hope for improvement.

A. Explain that *the focus of treatment will be on interpersonal interactions in the patient's daily life* rather than on dreams, cognitions, homework, etc.; and rather than on the patient's past trauma. You will be meeting once a week, which is important to maintain momentum; and each week you'll be asking about how the patient has been feeling, what has been happening in the patient's life, and how those two aspects of the patient's life interconnect.

B. You can explain that *there is no homework in IPT*—you will not be giving the patient assignments. The goal of treatment will be to resolve the patient's current interpersonal life crisis and thereby resolve the PTSD symptoms. Many patients may be relieved that you will not be asking them to do things they may not want to do. (Although there is no explicit homework, there is in fact the implicit task that the patient will need to resolve the interpersonal problem area by the end of the time-limited therapy. The patient can of course choose the pace at which to do this.) Despite not assigning homework, you will gently encourage the patient to take risks—not truly dangerous risks (about which patients with PTSD will surely be wary), but healthy endeavors that may feel emotionally risky—in order to help the patient make interpersonal changes necessary to resolve his or her symptoms.

For example: "This is actually a great time to risk changing certain behaviors that are getting in your way: If you try something out that goes well, you're likely to feel better. If you try something new and it doesn't work, that would be disappointing, but even then we could review what went wrong and learn from it. So I'm going to encourage you to 'live dangerously.'"

C. *Give the patient the sick role* (Parsons, 1951), excusing the patient from self-blame for symptoms of PTSD and what PTSD prevents him or her from doing. Encourage the patient to *blame the illness*, or the current interpersonal situation, rather than him- or herself. This is especially important with victims of childhood physical or sexual abuse, who often blame themselves rather than their attackers. Patients often feel crazy, damaged, and out of control. The very strength of the feelings they are attempting to suppress can contribute to that feeling. It can be reassuring to hear that PTSD is a serious but treatable illness, and that the sick role may only be temporary.

"Because you have PTSD—all the symptoms that we've gone over— you are not functioning at your best. It's hard to do things when you're anxious, having trouble concentrating, and on high alert. It's hard to read other people's behavior when you're feeling numb and detached. It's not your fault: like when you have the flu, you just have to adjust for symptoms that get in the way. Do the best you can, and don't blame yourself; blame the PTSD. As you get better, the PTSD symptoms should get in your way less and less."

D. *Set a time limit.* The patient needs to know that treatment is not open-ended. The time limit pressures both the patient and you to move forward, and is probably an active ingredient in the treatment (see Chapter 3). Explain that there is now good evidence that 14 weekly sessions of IPT often relieve the symptoms of PTSD. You will meet once a week, ideally at the same time (so that the patient has a regular, expectable schedule). By suggesting that things may improve in a matter of weeks, the time limit helpfully challenges the patient's expectation that this chronic condition will continue indefinitely.

Although the time limit is a therapist-imposed fiction that you can always alter if you must, it's important for you as a therapist to hold to it, to keep the pressure on the patient for change. Don't spread sessions out over multiple weeks if you can help it. Try to make up missed appointments in the same week to maintain continuity. If a patient misses multiple appointments, blame the PTSD rather than the patient, but continue counting down the weeks to termination, holding to the original contract, so that the time pressure does not weaken.

E. *Contingencies.*
   - Make sure that the patient has a way to contact you in an emergency. You want to make yourself available to patients, within reason:

   "If you're feeling worse, please give me a call. I'd rather know what's going on than not know."

A statement like this communicates your interest, concern, and availability. In our experience, patients with PTSD tend to underuse rather than overuse this privilege.

   - Try to let the patient know in advance if you will be away from the office on vacation, and what backup care will be available in that circumstance. Be prompt to sessions, providing an expectable, unalarming environment.
   - If the patient cancels a session, or you have to miss a session, do your best to try to make up the session in the same week. Once-weekly sessions provide a thematic continuity and regular interpersonal contact that give the therapy a rhythm and momentum. It's a good

interval for which the patient can answer the question, "How have
things been since we last met?"

- You can give the patient an IPT-PTSD informational handout to help
cement understanding of the PTSD diagnosis and of how therapy is
likely to proceed. (See Appendix.)
- Ask the patient if these arrangements make sense and are agreeable.
Encourage the patient to bring up anything else that's bothering him
or her.

PHASE 3: INITIAL SYMPTOMATIC RELIEF

Once you have diagnosed the patient's disorder(s) and the interpersonal
context of the PTSD, linked them in a formulation that the patient has accepted, and laid out the parameters of treatment, IPT enters its middle phase.
Interestingly, just doing this diagnostic preparatory work tends to calm patients and to generate the beginnings of a treatment alliance. We have not
repeated CAPS scores for PTSD patients after two or three sessions, but my
bet would be that they slightly decrease. Patients don't fully trust you, and
they continue to suffer, but they derive some hope from experiencing the IPT
therapist's organized and collaborative approach, and they suffer a little less.
Sometimes patients will report that a comment during the session has relieved
them: "It really helped when you said that what happened to me wasn't my
fault and is treatable." Providing a rational structure for treatment itself has
benefit. This decrement in distress provides some momentum for the therapy
to continue and build.

Other Aspects of Treatment

Like any effective treatment, IPT depends on the so-called *common factors*
shared across psychotherapies (Frank, 1971; Wampold, 2001; Barnicot et al.,
2014) (Table 5.1). These factors help in establishing a strong *therapeutic alliance*, which has been shown to be crucial in the outcome of all treatments,
including not only psychotherapy but pharmacotherapy as well (Krupnick et
al., 1996). To build an alliance, you need to be a good and sympathetic listener,
helping the patient feel understood. Let feelings, including painful feelings,
build in sessions before intervening—don't cut them off because they're uncomfortable, a maneuver that may further the patient's view of negative affects
as dangerous. Normalize feelings *as* feelings: emotions are reactions to interpersonal encounters, and patients may appropriately feel angry if someone has

Table 5.1. THE COMMON FACTORS OF PSYCHOTHERAPY

- Affective arousal (Response)
- Feeling understood by therapist (Relationship)
- Framework for understanding (Rationale)
- Expertise (Reassurance)
- Therapeutic procedure (Ritual)
- Optimism for improvement (Realistic)
- Success experiences (Remoralization)

NOTE: Adapted from Frank, J. (1971). Therapeutic factors in psychotherapy. *American Journal of Psychotherapy, 25,* 350–361.

wronged them, sad if someone has disappointed them or is leaving, and happy if things go'well. Underscore the feelings and link them to the patient's situation. Try to be flexible about appointments, make up time if a patient comes late when possible. Be supportive, encouraging, understanding, nonjudgemental. All of these common factors constitute aspects of good therapy, and IPT encourages using all of them fully. (Not all psychotherapies may use all common factors equally [Markowitz & Milrod, 2011].)

- For patients with PTSD, affective arousal is particularly important. Affective arousal makes sessions meaningful rather than dry and intellectualized; patients remember things that happen in emotional sessions, and they have the chance to experience powerful emotions as less "dangerous" than they have previously considered them to be.
- Focusing on specific, affectively charged current events is a great way to elicit feelings and the problems the patient is having. It keeps the therapy engaging, rather than letting it slide off into intellectualized abstractions.
- The IPT link between emotions and life events offers a framework that makes sense to patients, perhaps especially so in the extreme context of PTSD. The framework helps patients feel understood.
- Your expertise and poise as a therapist provides reassurance.
- The therapeutic procedure provides a workable, useful, and predictable method for understanding feelings and improving interpersonal functioning, two key areas of life functioning that again have particular import for patients with PTSD.
- IPT therapists provide optimism for improvement (based on empirical results).
- IPT provides success experiences—achievements of mastery for patients who feel weak, inadequate, overwhelmed, helpless, and

fragile—in the forms of both better understanding of their feelings
and the ability to use them to improve interpersonal encounters and
to resolve their presenting life crisis.

For these patients, *normalizing negative affects* is crucial. What patients may
see as "bad" or inappropriate feelings are often appropriate and useful signals. Anger may be an appropriate response to a provocation or attack. It's
not "mean" or aggressive to defend oneself against an attack; it's self-defense.
A little selfishness is healthy, not "selfish" in a bad, overweening way; if you
don't express your needs, you're unlikely to get them met. Being assertive is
not the same thing as being pushy or aggressive: it's simply expressing one's
needs and desires. Helping patients understand such feelings as social signals
is a gift beyond that of symptomatic response. It gives patients a different and
more comfortable way of looking at themselves, relationships, and the world.

The patients you treat will have survived horrific events and deserve caring
attention. At the same time, no matter how bad their experience, you can
provide therapeutic optimism: they *have* survived, they can grow from the
painful experience, this is a chance for them to recover their lives. (The idea
of being a *survivor*, and in some ways stronger for it, is one positive aspect
that can be used in reframing a posttraumatic role transition.) Our preliminary study (Bleiberg & Markowitz, 2005) showed that IPT helped badly, multiply, and chronically traumatized patients, so there was reason to believe it
would help patients in the randomized controlled trial. It worked there, too
(Markowitz et al., 2015). IPT also encourages the kind of *success experiences*
that help patients feel they have more control over their lives, and that help
patients get better.

While in the role of caring ally, you want to focus treatment on the patient's
current life and relationships *outside* the office, not on your relationship with
the patient itself.

Psychoeducation, a process that may proceed throughout treatment, should
leave the patient with an understanding of PTSD and its treatment. It should
begin in the first session as part of the discussion of what PTSD means. Don't
go into long-winded speeches about this: provide information at judicious moments, in digestible packets. The IPT-PTSD handout (see Appendix) can reinforce this process. Psychoeducation involves several points:

A. First, PTSD is a disorder, but it's an understandable response to a
   dreadfully upsetting trauma. If you're hurt badly enough, you withdraw, hunker down, and just try to survive. Suppressing emotion
   may be necessary for immediate survival, as may hypervigilance.
   Unfortunately, such behavior may persist long past its point of

Table 5.2. TASKS OF THE INITIAL PHASE OF IPT-PTSD

- **Diagnose** PTSD
- Diagnose the interpersonal context: take an **interpersonal inventory**
- Link them in a **formulation**, and get the patient's explicit agreement
- Consider pharmacotherapy
- Give the patient the **sick role**
- Set the **time limit**
- Set the **framework** for treatment
- Begin sessions with: **"How have things been since we last met?"**
- Provide **psychoeducation**
- Address contingencies

usefulness. As the patient comes to terms with life after the trauma, he or she can (re)gain a social equilibrium and feel better. Having a treatable diagnosis is not nearly so bad as feeling that there is something inherently defective about you as a person.

B. It is helpful for the patient to understand the emotional, physical, and cognitive *symptoms* of PTSD. You may review these with the patient by reading the diagnostic criteria section of the *DSM-5* (American Psychiatric Association, 2013, pp. 271–272; Chapter 2, Table 2.1 of this book) together. Repeating the CAPS interview or other symptom severity ratings periodically during the treatment will also reinforce the nature of the symptoms. Reviewing the social consequences of PTSD—damaged relationships, etc.—is crucial from the IPT perspective.

C. The patient may also be reassured that PTSD is *treatable*. A number of treatments work. IPT has done very well so far. Even symptoms that IPT does not directly address (e.g., flashbacks) tend to improve as the syndrome responds to IPT. You can't promise that IPT will help the patient—no treatment works for everyone—but you are optimistic that you can help the patient regain his or her life after this tragedy. Even if IPT should not work, there are alternative psychotherapies and medications that may address the symptoms. There is clinical *hope*.

The goal of this initial phase of IPT is to complete the history-taking and to set the framework for the treatment as efficiently as possible, so that a maximal amount of time remains to actually treat the disorder in the middle phase. The more socially uncomfortable, anxious, disorganized, or mistrustful your patient is, the longer it is likely to take to gather a history and to establish the basic therapeutic alliance needed to proceed. Table 5.2 summarizes the tasks of this phase.

6

IPT for PTSD—Middle Phase

"My tongue will tell the anger of my heart
Or else my heart, concealing it, will break. ..."
                —SHAKESPEARE, *The Taming of the Shrew, IV, 3*

Once you have obtained the patient's explicit agreement to the formulation, you enter the second phase of treatment. This comprises roughly sessions 4–11. You and the patient focus on the interpersonal problem area (*grief, role transition,* or *role dispute*) in order to try to improve the patient's emotional read of interpersonal encounters and the patient's interpersonal functioning. Successful experiences in handling social situations (e.g., a successful encounter with a co-worker or family member) are likely to give the patient a greater sense of control over the environment, and symptomatic relief. The IPT manual (Weissman et al., 2007) describes specific goals and strategies for each of the problem areas. These do not meaningfully differ in their application to PTSD.

For *grief (complicated bereavement)*, the goals include facilitating mourning (catharsis) and finding new relationships and activities to fill the void that the death of a significant other has left. Whereas bereavement itself is not a psychiatric disorder, complicated bereavement is. Symptoms may include those atypical of usual grief, such as excessive guilt and suicidal ideation. The death of a significant other may be associated with uncomfortably ambivalent feelings about the other person and the lost relationship, leading the patient either not to grieve at all or to take on the role of a chronic professional mourner, too guilty to see a moment of calm or pleasure as anything but a betrayal of the deceased. Neither of these stances is adaptive.

As in IPT for major depressive disorder, IPT for grief in PTSD explores the patient's feelings, positive and negative, about the lost person. The cause of death is likely to be related to (or may be) the traumatic event defining the patient's syndrome. Rather than focusing on the trauma *per se*, the therapist focuses on the relationship. It is usually easier for patients initially to describe what they liked and what they miss about the lost person and relationship. The therapist pulls for affect, and gradually explores and validates less positive feelings as well. The message is: It's okay, even natural, to dislike or hate someone who has died; it's expectable to have mixed feelings about people, perhaps especially the people you are close to. And talking about your feelings may be painful, but it isn't dangerous, and dealing with them may prove a relief.

As these feelings emerge, *it is important for you to resist the anxious temptation to interrupt powerful emotions: your job is to model for the patient that strong feelings are tolerable, understandable, and will pass.* The patient generally experiences catharsis in dealing with the loss and understands it more fully. At the same time, therapist and patient work on how the patient is handling interpersonal encounters in current daily life and how PTSD may be adversely influencing them. Patients, who typically feel adrift after the traumatic death of a loved one, need to find a new direction and substitute relationships, and generally begin to accomplish this during the course of treatment.

In a *role dispute*, the patient is overtly or covertly struggling with a significant other: a spouse, family member, friend, boss, or co-worker. Frequently this is a consequence of, or at least exacerbated by, the traumatic event. Therapist and patient determine whether or not the relationship is truly at an impasse (as the patient generally perceives it to be), and whether there are interpersonal strategies the patient can use to resolve it. What is the dispute? What does the patient want? What has he or she tried to do to resolve it? What else can be done?

The reason IPT calls these interpersonal conflicts "role disputes" is that they contain a distortion of the axiom that good relationships are based on bilateral compromise. No two people agree on everything, so each compromises to some degree for the other, hopefully in a balanced *quid pro quo*. In some relationships, however, this relationship becomes polarized: one person may demand satisfaction of his or her needs, and the other may provide that satisfaction at undue cost to his or her own. You can see how a depressed or anxious patient, feeling inadequate, unlovable, and burdensome, might have trouble asserting his or her needs and denying those of another person. Yet patients suffer, often feeling resentful and unappreciated—but helpless—in such relationships. IPT helps such patients by first eliciting and validating their wishes and dislikes, then using role play to prepare the patient for trying to *renegotiate the relationship into a fairer balance.* The goal of IPT becomes an attempt to improve the role dispute or else, failing that, ultimately to end it, which precipitates a role transition. Role disputes, which are conducted almost as unilateral couples therapy, are excellent opportunities for developing or redeveloping social skills.

In a *role transition*, the patient needs to recognize that *what feels like chaos is a transition*; then mourn the loss of the old role and relinquish it, while recognizing and adapting to the potentials of the new role. We have found that even patients who suffer objectively bad events (notably, learning that they have HIV infection [Markowitz et al., 1998]) can come to see the bright side of such transitions. Role transitions are inherent in PTSD: a distressing life event has occurred, after which a patient views life differently, and for the worse, and after which he or she has developed the symptoms and interpersonal difficulties of PTSD. Again, treatment focuses on the interpersonal consequences of the loss/change and how the patient can regain social supports and interpersonal competence.

As previously noted, the fourth interpersonal focus, *interpersonal deficits*, defines patients who lack life events. This is the least well defined IPT category and carries the poorest prognosis. An advantage of treating patients with PTSD is that, because they have by definition a defining life event, this category can be avoided altogether.

Patients with PTSD, like many patients with major depression or dysthymic disorder, often feel that feelings like anger are "bad," and have trouble expressing or even acknowledging them. Yet such affects are inevitable human responses, and they potentially inform patients of what is happening in their interpersonal situations. They frequently arise during role disputes. People feel angry when they have been attacked or offended; ignoring or suppressing this feeling often leaves them feeling anxious and uncomfortable. Moreover, the interaction with the other person has ended uncomfortably, and whoever is bothering them will receive no cue from the patient that their behavior is hurtful and unacceptable. The undesired interpersonal pattern is therefore likely to continue.

Therapists should *elicit* the patient's feelings in such situations, *validate* and *normalize* them, *explore options for expressing them* (verbally), and *role play* them. Taking this one step at a time is important; don't rush to explore options until the patient has tolerated and recognized the feelings. As a therapist, you don't want to communicate the idea that feelings need to be avoided, that you or the patient should rapidly move on when a strong affect is uncovered. Better to sit with feelings, to tolerate (demonstrating that they are not dangerous) and to understand them.

One concept that is sometimes helpful is the idea of a *transgression* (Weissman et al., 2007). Certain behaviors break social codes, written or unwritten societal laws. Under such circumstances, *anyone* who has been transgressed against has a right to feel angry; anyone is entitled to an apology (if not greater recompense). Examples of transgressions include rudeness, betrayal, lying, violence, and so forth. The concept of a transgression—of a universally accepted violation—may help cautious, passive patients to feel that social law supports them. This may be an important reframing in encouraging them to confront transgressors, renegotiating a maladaptive relationship.

STRUCTURE OF SESSIONS

1. *Opening gambit.* Each session after the initial one begins with the question: *"How have things been since we last met?"* This elicits an interval history and focuses the patient on recent life events and associated affects. Exploring these helps patients connect feelings with life functioning. If the patient answers the question with an event from the interval between sessions, the therapist then asks how this affected the patient's feelings and symptoms. Alternatively, if the patient has answered the initial question with a mood or symptom change, the therapist asks about events. Thus, after two opening questions, the therapist and patient have identified an affectively charged recent event to discuss. This is an excellent substrate for good psychotherapy, and it is the substance of IPT.

2. *What happened?* The next step is to explore what happened. Where did things go right or wrong? What did the patient want to happen in that situation? How did the patient feel? When patients report success in an interpersonal encounter, the therapist provides *support* and *reinforcement.* ("Great job! . . . How did you feel after you did that?") If the patient has suffered a setback, the therapist offers sympathy; therapist and patient then explore how current PTSD symptoms interfered with the encounters (and how these encounters in turn perpetuate such symptoms).

In reconstructing what is often a minor interpersonal encounter—albeit one with an emotional impact on the patient's mood, suffering, and confidence—try to help the patient organize what has happened, essentially reconstructing a transcript of the experience.

"What did you say? . . . What did [s]he say? . . . Then how did you feel? . . . Then what did you say?"

Repeat this interrogatory triad (what IPT technically calls *communication analysis*) as often as needed to reconstruct the encounter. The information you gather can help both your and the patient's understanding on several levels:

1. It should give you a sense of how the patient interacts moment to moment in an interpersonal exchange with a potentially important family member, friend, or co-worker. Over time, these vignettes from the patient's life will add up to a much more detailed and accurate picture of the patient's interpersonal behavior than any generalizations the patient can provide.

2. Just recognizing the feelings that come up may be difficult for patients at first, due to the numbness and emotional avoidance of PTSD. This experience of recounting interpersonal interactions thus provides a crucial experience in affective attunement.
   "What did you feel when he said that? ... Upset? ... What kind of upset? What do you call that feeling?"

Gradually the patient may be able to distinguish among uncomfortable negative affects such as anger, sadness, and anxiety, all of which can tell you and the patient different things about what is happening in the interpersonal encounter the patient is describing. This builds an important emotional vocabulary, a considerable accomplishment and a necessity for coping in the patient's future interpersonal life.

3. You can listen for dissonances and discrepancies between how the patient reports feeling in the encounter ("How did you feel?") and what the patient then says ("Then what did you say?") to the other person. For example, did the patient feel angry but say nothing? We might expect that pattern as a consequence of PTSD. Such behavior often leaves patients anxiously uncomfortable, and anger may subsequently boil over in a different, trivial, or inappropriate setting, which only leads the patient to conclude that his or her feelings are out of control and need to be suppressed still more severely. Meanwhile, by not expressing feelings during the interchange you are examining, the patient is not informing the other person of what he or she wants or does not want, thereby perpetuating a role dispute. Thus, pursuing how the patient feels in an encounter is important in its own right, but any disconnection between what the patient feels and says has additional import. IPT works on *validating the feelings* so as to encourage their expression, thereby clarifying a future interchange and giving the patient a sense of mastery and control over what happens.

4. *Tolerating affect.* The above process allows what IPT calls *communication analysis*. It should make clear what has happened in the reported interaction and how the patient has felt and behaved in it. It should also allow you to help normalize the patient's emotional responses to interpersonal encounters. This affective attunement plays an important role in IPT generally, but a particularly large role in IPT for PTSD, where patients are likely to describe numbness or no feeling, and to associate strong feelings with danger. Again, you can model for the patient in sessions that *strong emotions, while uncomfortable, are not*

dangerous, and will pass if the patient just sits with them. Moreover, feelings are crucial emotional guideposts about what is happening in relationships, whom patients can trust or cannot trust. So while you may feel tempted—especially if a strong affect has arisen in the room—to move on to exploring options, don't rush.

Let the patient sit with the feeling long enough to recognize that it's meaningful, not toxic. (A behaviorist might argue that this is a form of exposure and habituation, and it is; but such exposure is far from the graded, systematic hierarchy of exposure exercises that constitute most behavioral therapies for PTSD.) An emotional session is generally a good session, even if it can feel exhausting. And it builds the reflective emotional capacity of the patient.

Your own emotional responses to the interpersonal encounters the patient describes should provide you with a template for responses. If you feel angry, or sad, or anxious on the patient's behalf—if that's how you would feel in that situation—that probably tells you something about a normative emotional response.

5. *Options*. Having established where things might have gone right or wrong in the encounter the patient is reporting, you as the therapist can support the patient's having risked the encounter in the first place, and reinforce any skills the patient has used adaptively in the encounter.

   "Brave of you to try. Are there parts of what happened that you're happy with?"

If the interchange has ended badly, you can sympathetically and supportively help the patient explore why:

   "Good that you tried. How did that feel? . . . I understand your disappointment about the way it ended. Where do you think things went wrong?"

Having normalized the patient's affective responses to the situation—having helped the patient recognize that a sad feeling reflected separation from a loved one, an angry feeling reflected perceived mistreatment—you can then explore *other options* the patient might use in the given situation:

   "What else could you try if that situation came up again?"

Patients may insist that they have no options, but that's almost never true. Even if options are few and difficult, they exist. Encourage the patient to come up with options rather than offering suggestions yourself: this will help the patient feel more competent. New options almost always exist, even if they're hard for a benumbed, anxious, and helpless-feeling patient to locate. Helpful options start with how the patient was feeling—say, angry—and your validation of anger as an appropriate social signal under the circumstances.

> "So *how* were you feeling at that point? ... And is it reasonable for you to have felt that way [given her behavior]?"

Some patients may need repeated, gentle (not overly didactic) psychoeducational reinforcement that it's okay to be angry if someone has offended you, and that the only way the other person will know they've offended you—and stop behaving that way—is if you tell them.

Feasible options often involve *verbalizing* the feelings that the patient has newly acknowledged, and the feelings that you have just helped the patient see as a reasonable, normal, meaningful emotional response. Frequently, this means asserting a wish ("I'd like to do this") or confronting a negative behavior ("It bothers me when you do that").

As treatment progresses, patients are increasingly likely to come to their session reporting positive encounters: interchanges where they have expressed their needs and received a positive response from others, or have confronted unwanted behavior and had the other person apologize or back off. When this happens, it's important to congratulate the patient, reinforcing adaptive behaviors; and to underscore the link between successful interpersonal behaviors and feeling better.

> "Great work! ... So how did you manage that? ... Do you feel comfortable using that approach in future?"

6. *Role play.* Once the patient has come up with a feasible option, you have the opportunity to *role play* so that the patient can rehearse it. It's often best to launch spontaneously into a role play, with you enacting the other person, rather than emphasizing the creation of an artificial situation by saying, "Let's role play." Use the situation and dialogue the patient has just provided to recreate the encounter. Hopefully the patient will take it in a new direction. Once the patient has done so, you can stop the role play and recapitulate it, eliciting the patient's reaction to both the *content* and the *tone*:
   "How did you feel [saying that]?"
   (That is, what was it like speaking in a more direct or assertive way?)
   "Did you say what you wanted to say?"

(If not, what would the patient add or say differently?)
"What about your tone of voice? How did you think you came across?"

Some patients worry that expressing anger shows that they're "mean" or "bad." Role plays give them the chance to practice modulating their tone, so that it's neither too deferential and meek nor too angry and explosive. Based on the patient's self-assessment of the role play, and judicious comments you might want to add (best stated in question form: "What did you think of the way you handled X?"), you can repeat the role play until the patient feels comfortable with the intervention.

It's also worth exploring contingencies. You might ask: "How is Mark likely to respond if you say that?"

The patient may come up with unexpected answers, which you can incorporate into subsequent role play. If the patient's partner has a tendency to get too angry, how can the patient respond to that? ("What options are available?" can lead to further role play.) The more contingencies you cover, the more practice the patient gets, and the more comfortable the patient is likely to feel turning role play into interpersonal action between sessions.

Therefore, whether the patient reports a positive or negative event and mood in response to the session's opening question, the session should lead to an exploration of interpersonal functioning and a strengthening of interpersonal skills. Even bad reported outcomes should result in constructive exploration and new plans. Do not hesitate to congratulate patients for achievements (they need that reinforcement) nor hesitate to sympathize with setbacks. Either intervention, if delivered with authentic feeling, helps build the therapeutic alliance. Recognize that the patient is suffering and that taking interpersonal risks is brave. No formal homework is assigned in IPT, but the framework of the treatment focus itself constitutes a task: e.g., the need to resolve a role transition in the time-limited therapy. Thus implicit in role play is the idea that the patient will want to use it, sooner or later, in life.

The focus of treatment therefore tends to rest on daily encounters with significant others or strangers: how the patient has handled an interaction with a family member, a friend, a co-worker, a doctor, or some man on the street or in a convenience store. Focus on the particular to elicit affect. Ask patients to name people in encounters rather than using anonymous pronouns. Ask for actual dialogue rather than summaries of exchanges. These small encounters provide an opportunity for the patient to express feelings and needs in a manner appropriate to the situation, which should make these encounters go better and leave the patient feeling that the world is safer and more manageable than PTSD has led him or her to believe. When these encounters go well, the therapist reinforces the patient's adaptive interpersonal skills, always making the link between mood and life events ("You handled that really well! So no wonder you're feeling a little better!").

The patient will return the next week, to be greeted by the same opening question. This should yield another interpersonal situation, hopefully linked to the central problem area, an update on the previous session. If the patient handled the situation well, he or she may be feeling better, and you can reinforce gains. If not, you can sympathize, re-strategize, and encourage the patient to keep working on the interpersonal issues. I encourage patients to "Live dangerously!"—not to take reckless chances, but to take appropriate interpersonal risks that may nonetheless feel dangerous at first.

To recap, the general progression in sessions should be as follows:

1. Identify a recent, affectively charged event and determine its outcome.
2. Elicit the patient's feelings in and about this event. Helping the patient name his or her feelings cultivates a useful skill. Again, don't interrupt powerful affects—let the patient experience strong emotions as useful, meaningful feelings before you intervene.
3. Validate those feelings. Usually you will be able to empathize and support the patient's feelings. The emotions an event elicits tend to be intuitively predictable. In the instance where a patient reports an odd or confusing reaction to an event, it is worth exploring the feelings, understanding the situation from the patient's perspective, and validating what you can in that reaction. If the patient brings up guilt or a PTSD-related response, you can label these as symptoms of the syndrome.
4. This depends upon how the reported encounter went:
   a. If things have gone well, *support the patient's adaptive interpersonal behaviors.* Congratulate the patient on successes. Cheerleading is okay so long as it's not forced and saccharine.
   b. If things have not gone well, *sympathize; elicit the patient's feelings* (don't trivialize or dismiss the event). Then, acknowledging that things haven't gone well, *explore alternative interpersonal options* with the patient. When you have settled on a feasible alternative, try to *role play* this with the patient. Usually this means jumping into a role play, letting the patient play him- or herself. Since patients may find role play artificial if you announce it as such, one useful way to slide into role play is to elicit the patient's feelings, then ask whether they might express them to the other person. Or ask, "So in your own mind (in fantasy), how might

you respond to that?" Before the patient realizes it, he or she is involved in role play.

5. *Thematic continuity* makes therapy feel coherent. Don't hammer home the idea of a complicated bereavement, role dispute, or role transition every few minutes (or even every session, necessarily). But reminding the patient, where appropriate, of how PTSD symptoms interfere with functioning, or of how the patient is maneuvering through a role dispute or role transition, may help tie things together. Sometimes the therapist can do this neatly in summarizing a session at its end.

THEMATIC ISSUES

Typical themes of IPT for PTSD include the ideas that emphasize resilience:

"Reclaim your life!"

"You've been through something awful and unpredictable, but you can have some control over your environment."

"You're a survivor."

(Primo Levi noted that his horrific experience at Auschwitz left him "more mature and stronger," and was a "rite of passage" [Levi, 2003].)

Reviewing interpersonal situations, exploring the patient's feelings and options for action in such situations, and testing out such options can help patients regain a sense of control over their interpersonal environments. Doing so allows an appropriate release of affect, gains in socialization, and a diminution of symptoms. As patients feel better, they may spontaneously attempt self-exposure, but this is not the focus of the treatment. The IPT therapist's supportive, encouraging stance is that the patient's past trauma is bad enough; it's *"adding insult to injury"* that the past is interfering with the patient's current ability to function in relationships and other interpersonal encounters.

In treating patients who report remote childhood traumas, situations where the patients truly had little control over their lives, it may be helpful to acknowledge the pain of that situation but to point out: *"That was then; this is now."* Now an adult, the patient has more control over interpersonal encounters and can handle them differently. This may be a helpful maneuver for redirecting a patient from the past to the present.

IPT treats PTSD by focusing on emotions and interpersonal circumstances, not by directly targeting the symptoms themselves. In recounting recent interpersonal encounters, a patient may report flashbacks or other symptoms. If so, you can remind the patient that these are symptoms of PTSD that will likely fade as the patient regains control of his or her interpersonal situation. (This is what our research found [Markowitz et al., 2015].) It may be worth pointing out that such symptoms often appear not randomly, but in connection with a stressful current life circumstance: e.g., going to meet a friend when feeling uncertain or mistrustful. Mood and life events interact, on a small as well as on a larger, traumatic level. As a therapist, you want to maintain an interpersonal thematic focus (rather than, for example, bringing up biological, cognitive, or other formulations of symptoms the patient may be experiencing).

The brief description above (elaborated upon in Weissman et al., 2007) should illustrate that IPT is a focused but not overly structured treatment. Its emphasis on feelings and social functioning explains why patients gain social skills in the course of IPT.

IPT therapists offer support, clarification, and realistic clinical optimism. They normalize the patient's feelings in an interpersonal context, and (aided by the time limit) encourage the patient to tackle and solve practical problems in everyday encounters with people in the patient's life. They take the role of a friendly ally, with a relatively relaxed and informal stance. They may offer occasional self-disclosure or advice when clinically warranted. They do *not* interpret dreams (if the patient offers a dream, the therapist can briefly help the patient explore its manifest interpersonal content), interpret transference (Markowitz et al., 1998a), assign behavioral homework, or formally encourage exposure to trauma reminders.

In our treatment studies, we told IPT therapists: *"Whereas you should not discourage a patient from spontaneously facing trauma reminders, you also should not encourage such behavior."* The goal of IPT in the research study is to test a *different* approach to treating PTSD than the standard exposure to reminders of trauma. IPT should focus on interpersonal encounters in the patient's current life, not on reconstructing, reliving, and facing reminders of past traumas.

7

IPT for PTSD—Role Transitions

"No tongue can tell, no mind conceive, no pen portray the horrible sights I witnessed this morning."
—UNION CAPTAIN JOHN TAGGERT, *9th Pennsylvania Reserves Antietam, September 17th, 1862*

You have to know when to let the old life go, and go on and not look back and have regrets, I always say. Otherwise you will be sad, because you are always losing something. That's the way life is, if you let misfortunes strike you too hard, you won't see the new chance coming.
—SUSAN SONTAG: *The Volcano Lover.* (New York: Picador, *1992, P. 402)*

Most IPT manuals work their way through the sequence of interpersonal problem areas by starting with complicated grief. In our randomized study, 40 patients were randomly assigned to IPT. Thirty-eight of them actually began treatment and agreed upon a treatment focus. Of those 38 patients, 30 (79%) were treated for role transitions. Because role transitions are the most common focal interpersonal problem area for patients with PTSD, we will start with them. This and the succeeding chapters will be built on case examples to illustrate the focal problem areas. All cases have been disguised to protect the confidentiality of patients.

CASE EXAMPLE 1

Martina, 25-year-old single white woman clerical worker, presented with more than four years of PTSD and major depression. Her chief complaint was: "I've been feeling weird, cut off." She had nearly been killed by debris from the World Trade Center, where she fortuitously had arrived late for her job and joined the walking exodus from downtown Manhattan. The destruction there put her out of work. A month later, in October 2001, she was mugged at knife point in the lobby of her apartment building. Her assailants stole her brief-case, which contained the only diskettes of the novel she had been working on for the previous two years. She met full *DSM-IV* criteria for PTSD, including flashbacks, hypervigilance, detachment, and suspiciousness of others. Her Clinician-Administered PTSD Scale (CAPS, Blake et al., 1995) score was 60, indicating severe PTSD (Weathers et al., 2001). She also met criteria for a mod-erately severe major depressive episode, scoring a 23 on the 24-item Hamilton Depression Rating Scale (Hamilton, 1960). She had trouble enjoying anything, felt frightened, felt that other people could not be trusted, that life was hope-less. She subsequently broke up with a boyfriend who she felt did not under-stand what she had been going through.

The therapist gathered this history in the first two sessions and collected an interpersonal inventory. Martina was the youngest of three sisters. She denied prior trauma. From childhood, she had generally been passive and avoidant in dealing with other people. She announced to the therapist that she had never liked confrontations, preferring to keep her feelings to her-self, and taking a rather passive, nonassertive role with others. She had friends, and occasional brief sexual encounters, but had always had diffi-culty getting close to other people. There was no one she thought of as a confidant.

She was an alert, quiet white woman appearing roughly her stated age, well groomed, dressed in rather conservative and drab clothing. Her movements were mildly agitated, her speech soft and hesitant, fluent and unpressured. She avoided eye contact. Her mood was anxious and depressed, with a constricted, minimally reactive affect. Her thoughts appeared goal-directed, if marked by ruminations about her failings ("I'm a weak person"). She reported passive su-icidal ideation without plans or intent. Sensorium was grossly clear.

In the context of her recent trauma, Martina reported having told and having received "some" support from her family members. Their response had been to listen briefly, cut her off, and tell her to buck up and get over it. She said that that was what she had expected, and denied having any emotional reaction to this interchange. She reported a similar interaction with her female roommate in their shared apartment. She nonetheless said she was left feeling alone and misunderstood. She withdrew from her few friends and kept a distance from co-workers at a new job she had found. She also made no attempt to write, felt that her life was over, and that a new disaster was surely waiting around the corner.

In session 3, Martina's therapist framed her situation as a role transition:

THERAPIST: You've given me a lot of helpful history. Can I ask you if
I understand what you've told me? You have been through not one
but two traumas, both life-threatening and extremely upsetting. As
a result of those traumas, you have a CAPS score of 60, which means
you have severe posttraumatic stress disorder. PTSD is a treatable
disorder, though, and you have a good chance of getting better in this
14-week treatment. And it's not your fault that this happened to you.
It's bad enough that you had to go through these terrible events, but
even worse that the PTSD is affecting your life day to day, making it
hard to enjoy things or interact with other people. It's left you more
isolated and unhappy, not knowing whom to trust. This brief therapy
is a chance to *reclaim your life*, not to be cheated by these two disasters
from living life to its fullest. We call what you've been through a *role
transition*: distressing things have happened that have changed your
life and your sense of whom you can trust. I suggest that we use the
remaining 11 sessions of this treatment to focus on how the PTSD is
interfering with your feelings and your relationships, so that you can
decide whom to trust and whom not to. Does that make sense to you?

It did. Thus they agreed on a formulation that defined the remainder of the
treatment. IPT focused not on Martina's traumas—which were never directly
mentioned again—but on the consequences of the traumas on her relationships. These, perhaps never strong, were further distanced in the context of
PTSD. The therapist set treatment as 14 consecutive 50-minute weekly sessions
and gave the patient the sick role:

No one is at her best after going through something like this. You've
been hit hard, and your symptom scores show it. You can expect
that it may be hard to function; give yourself a break for what you
don't feel up to, just as you would if you had the flu. In fact, PTSD is
a lot worse than the flu. As we work on these issues, you're likely to
gradually feel better and to function better. We'll be repeating the
rating scales at regular intervals to make sure you are getting better.

With their agreement on the formulation, Martina and her therapist entered
the middle phase of IPT. Martina continued to appear agitated and hesitant,
acknowledging some anxiety and depression but otherwise reporting detachment from her feelings. The therapist began each session asking,

"How have things been since we last met?"

This tended to elicit minor daily events, mainly at work, inasmuch as Martina's always impoverished social life had atrophied in the setting of PTSD. The therapist then asked:

"And how did that make you feel?"

MARTINA: I don't know. I didn't feel anything. . . . Maybe a little upset.

The therapist would then explore: "What kind of upset? . . . What do you call that feeling?"
And, having elicited it: "Does it make sense, is that a reasonable feeling to have had?"

It turned out that Martina did have one friend at her job, Jamie, who went on a week's vacation a few weeks into the therapy. Martina had agreed to cover her which entailed doubling her work load. Jamie then called at the end of the week, asking if Martina could cover for a second week. Martina acquiesced. In discussing this in therapy, she said it was "no big deal." When, at the end of the second week, the friend called and asked for yet another week of coverage, Martina began to feel taken advantage of.

MARTINA: I want to be nice to her, but I'm starting to feel a little uncomfortable about this. [Silence]
THERAPIST: Tell me.
MARTINA: Well, she seemed nice at work, and I wanted to be nice, too, but I've been working overtime for her and she doesn't really seem to notice, to appreciate it.
THERAPIST: It does seem that way. So what feelings does that bring up?
MARTINA: Oh, nothing. I don't know.
THERAPIST: [raises eyebrows and waits]
MARTINA: I guess it bothers me a little.
THERAPIST: What do you call that feeling?
MARTINA: I guess I'm a little frustrated, a little . . . annoyed.
THERAPIST: Huh. And does that seem a reasonable reaction, with Jamie asking for more and more and not seeming to notice what it means for you?
MARTINA: . . . Yes, I guess. I'm a little bit mad at her. But I don't like that feeling. Never have.
THERAPIST: Tell me about that.
MARTINA: I just don't feel comfortable. I feel like I'm mean, not a good person.
THERAPIST: Are you feeling that frustration/anger out of the blue, or do you think there's a reason for it?

They discussed whether Jamie had transgressed good behavior, "stepped over the line" in asking a little too much of Martina. The therapist worked to normalize the feeling:

> THERAPIST: Maybe if you get angry at someone for no reason, that's being mean. But often anger is a useful social signal, it tells you that someone else is misbehaving. In a way, that's how you *know* someone's not treating you well: you feel annoyed or angry.
> MARTINA: I'm not very comfortable with this.
> THERAPIST: Everyone's a little uncomfortable about anger, and PTSD makes it still harder to deal with—strong "negative" emotions like anger can feel overwhelming. But we're trying to focus on whom you can trust, and this is one way to figure it out.

Having normalized the anger, the therapist asked what Martina could do with it:

> THERAPIST: So your feelings are telling you something about how Jamie's behaving—or misbehaving. What can you *do* about it? . . . What options do you have?
> MARTINA: I don't know. I don't think there's anything I can do.
> THERAPIST: [silent]
> MARTINA: I guess I can just give up on her as a friend.
> THERAPIST: That's certainly one option. But you've said that Jamie's the person you've been friendliest with at work. Before you give up on her, do you have any other options?

With a little gentle prodding, they came around to the idea that Martina could put her feelings into words.

> MARTINA: I guess I could say something. . . .
> THERAPIST: Good idea! You could put your feelings into words. What might you say?
> MARTINA: I don't know, I'm uncomfortable. . . . "Jamie, it's not that I don't want you to enjoy your vacations, but maybe you didn't realize what all these extra days meant for me. It's been a little hard."
> THERAPIST [after waiting to see whether she would continue]: How did that sound? Did you say what you wanted to say?
> MARTINA: Let me try again. "Jamie, I didn't resent your being away at first, but with all these extensions I felt a little—taken advantage of. I feel . . . like you haven't really been paying attention to how I feel."

THERAPIST: How did that sound? How did that feel?

MARTINA: Better.

THERAPIST: How did you feel about your tone—did you come across the way you wanted to?

MARTINA: I don't know, maybe it wasn't strong enough.

THERAPIST: Let's try it again. . . .

After a time they reached a more comfortable role play, with Martina cautiously showing more affect.

THERAPIST: So this is a great step. If you tell Jamie how you feel and she blows you off, it may mean you can't trust her and that it makes sense to give up your friendship. On the other hand, if she hears you, and maybe apologizes, perhaps you can trust her and continue your friendship.

MARTINA: That makes sense.

There was no follow-up to this in the following session, in which Martina talked about her roommate and a minor incident with her family. The therapist had been hoping Martina would confront Jamie, but recognized that things would happen at Martina's pace. The next session:

THERAPIST: How have things been since we last met?

MARTINA: Actually, a little better.

THERAPIST: Good to hear. Did something happen that contributed to your feeling better?

MARTINA: Actually, yes. You know, we had talked about my talking to Jamie, who finally came back to work. I was nervous about doing it, and I actually wasn't going to bring it up, but we got into a conversation about something else, and it happened.

THERAPIST: What happened?

MARTINA: Well, I felt a little annoyed with her not even mentioning my having covered her for so long, and I finally said something. It wasn't exactly what we had rehearsed, but it was close enough. And—and I said, "I think maybe you owe me an apology." Then I was really nervous, and she looked at me. But then she said, "You know, you're right. I'm sorry. I guess I took advantage of your good nature."

THERAPIST: Wow! How did you feel?

MARTINA: It felt great having taken the chance to say something, and especially that she heard me and acknowledged I was right. I felt better. . . . I do feel like we can stay friends.

THERAPIST: Great work! Brave of you to take the risk, and it sounds like it really paid off. So maybe you can trust your feelings, and even put them into words to see whether you can trust people in your life?
MARTINA: Maybe.

Martina seemed much less symptomatic and more open after this point. A session or two later, she reported that her gynecologist had treated her brusquely during an examination in which she felt vulnerable and hurt. The doctor had explained his procedures, and Martina had not spoken up about how bad she felt—it was all an anxious, detached blur. In the session, the IPT therapist again validated her feelings of hurt and anger, explored potential responses, and role-played them with her. Martina reported that the next day she called up the doctor, arranged a follow-up appointment, and—somewhat to her own surprise, since she felt this was out of character—expressed her grievances. To her further surprise, the doctor apologized.

THERAPIST: How have things been since we last met?
MARTINA: Better, and let me tell you why!

Following this incident, symptoms further decreased, presumably reflecting Martina's greater sense of agency and control over her environment. Based on these successes, she took further interpersonal risks; for example, telling family members more about how she had felt unsupported when she had previously spoken to them about her traumas. In each instance, thankfully, Martina received contrite responses from the other party she confronted. As a therapist, one hopes for such good outcomes. Her therapist had, however, reviewed contingencies with her in each case: "How will you handle it if they aren't apologetic? What options do you have?"—and they had role-played these so that Martina would have been prepared had things not gone so smoothly.

Based on these successful encounters, Martina felt increasingly competent in social circumstances. She was struck by the sense that her feelings were just and meaningful, and that she could use them to assert herself with other people. She opened up to her roommate, turning a somewhat distant living situation into a friendship. By the end of treatment, she felt she was doing this better than she ever had before—even before the September 11th trauma. Both PTSD and major depression resolved: her CAPS score had fallen to 17 and her Hamilton Depression Rating Scale score to 4. She applied for and was awaiting a promotion at work, resumed her writing, and rebuilt her social connections. She had tentatively resumed dating, and felt she was handling such dating better, as therapy ended.

Termination, in sessions 12–14, was "a mixed bag," in her words. On one hand, Martina was flying high with a sense of new social competence. She was also literally flying: after having avoided airplanes since the September 11th trauma, she spontaneously took one to go on a vacation, mentioning the trip to the therapist only after having ticketed it. On the other hand, she initially worried that she was feeling depressed. On discussion, however, she and her therapist agreed that she was feeling *sad*—without neurovegetative symptoms, guilt, or suicidal ideation—at the prospect of ending therapy. Her therapist normalized sadness as the emotion of parting and loss: normal, and not at all the same thing as depression, although the feelings can overlap. Martina baked a cake for her final session, and thanked her therapist for "practically saving my life." At six months follow-up, she remained well, was in a relationship, had gotten her promotion, and did not feel the need for further therapy.

Note how differently this IPT treatment evolved than would an exposure-based treatment. There was no discussion of the trauma after the initial session, and only brief discussion then. There was no attempt to make Martina reconstruct the traumatic events and confront reminders that evoked them. Instead, IPT focused on helping Martina identify her feelings and use them in current interpersonal relationships. By gaining a greater sense of mastery of her inner emotions and outside relationships, and of the connection between them, Martina also managed to shed her re-experiencing, avoidance, and other symptoms of PTSD.

CASE EXAMPLE 2

Chuck, a 34-year-old married Catholic veteran engineer, presented with PTSD related to combat in the Middle East. His chief complaint was: "I haven't gotten over Iraq, and my wife is driving me crazy." On his second tour of duty, Chuck reported that his armored vehicle had hit an improvised explosive device (IED) in Fallujah, and that he had seen his company buddies and some "other people" (presumably civilians) die in Iraq. Although his physical injuries were minor, the war had taken a toll. An honorably discharged Marine, Chuck reported experiencing flashbacks of explosions driving through the streets of New York. He awoke every night from horrible combat nightmares in which he was killing people or dying.

Life back home felt unreal; he felt numb, detached, and fearful; frightened of others. This included his wife, two young children, and relatives, who "can't understand, don't have a clue where I've been at." He had trouble driving, always fearing an explosion on the road. He was angry at the way the service had treated him and his comrades, how "the brass" and the politicians had mishandled the war. He came to treatment at our hospital because he mistrusted the Veterans Administration. Chuck had a CAPS score of 85, indicating extreme PTSD, and met *DSM-IV* criteria for paranoid personality disorder on the Structured Clinical Interview for *DSM-IV* Personality Disorders (SCID-II) interview. He initially reported carrying a knife, although he said he only planned to use it in self-defense. He was moderately depressed and reported moderate, sporadic alcohol abuse, with occasional blackouts, denying other drug use.

Chuck was employed, but he mistrusted his co-workers and appeared to be in difficulty at work because of his wary attitude. He reported his wife was longsuffering and tried to support him, but he found her "clueless" and unhelpful, unable to understand what he had gone through. He had not, however, tried to talk to her about his war experiences or his difficulties in reassimilating to civilian life. He reported having had a few angry "explosions" at home, and worked hard to avoid showing anger there and at work. He had a few Marine buddies he talked to by phone or text, who reported similar difficulty in adjusting to their return home. They were a band of brothers misunderstood by all around them.

Chuck arrived early for all of his sessions. On initial presentation, he was a muscular, fit-looking man appearing roughly his stated age, with a buzz cut and a scraggly moustache. A "Semper Fi" tattoo on a powerful bicep peeked out beneath his white T-shirt. He sat tensely in his chair, showed agitation at moments, and made wary, steady eye contact. His speech was fluent, measured, unpressured, with an often military cadence. His mood was anxious, mildly depressed, angry at moments, with a barely controlled, mildly labile, but generally detached and distanced affect. Thinking appeared grossly goal-directed, albeit with apparent ruminations, and paranoid thinking that nearly approached the level of delusions: his co-workers plotted against him, the neighbors might be listening in. He denied frank psychotic symptoms. He acknowledged moments of wanting to be dead or to hurt his oppressors, but said he prided himself on his control and would never act on these impulses. His sensorium was clear.

The first issue with a patient like this is to consider his paranoid stance. Recognizing the difficulty in diagnosing personality disorders in the context of Axis I disorders like major depression and PTSD, IPT therapists do not prejudge personality disorder until the Axis I disorder has been thoroughly treated. What could be more reasonable than that a veteran traumatized in a war would mistrust his surroundings (and his overwhelming internal emotional turmoil)? Hence we do not prejudge personality disorder until the Axis I disorder has been vigorously treated. Moreover, in our randomized trial, 28% of patients with chronic PTSD met SCID-II criteria for paranoid personality disorder at baseline; it was the most prevalent Axis II diagnosis. A mere 14 weeks later, however, 10 of 19 patients who had carried that personality disorder diagnosis, a full 53%, no longer did (Markowitz et al., 2015b). This rapid resolution of an apparent personality disorder surely justifies a "watch and wait" diagnostic stance. On the other hand, a clinician would be unwise to ignore a patient's interpersonal behavior in and outside the office. In IPT, characteristically, the therapist notes the behavior but attributes it to the traumatic event (and/or to the patient's current environment). Chuck's therapist confronted it gently but directly.

> THERAPIST: After what you went through in Iraq, it's hard for you to
> trust anything or anyone. I don't really expect you to trust me at
> first, either. When we meet, I'm not going to be trying to surprise
> or frighten you, or to push you to do anything you don't want to do.
> So if something comes up in our treatment that annoys or bothers
> you, or makes you anxious, please tell me. I won't be offended; on the
> contrary, it's just the kind of issue I'd love to discuss. Your feelings—
> annoyance, anger, anxiety—tell you something about what's going
> on with other people. . . . As you start to feel better, it may become
> clearer whom you can trust and not trust, and you will be able to feel
> more control over your situation and the people in it.

Chuck grunted assent. Throughout the treatment, the therapist was careful to ask Chuck's permission at every juncture, lest he feel threatened or manipulated. This was not someone to tell what to do, but rather to ask, to support his competence.

The therapist also suggested that Chuck minimize alcohol use—alcohol lowered anxiety in the short run but could make his mood and anxiety worse and his behavior feel more out of control. It was also clear that Chuck was struggling to ward off powerful internal feelings. Towards the end of the third session, the therapist incorporated this into a *formulation*:

> THERAPIST: You've given me a lot of helpful information, and I know
> that it hasn't always been easy. Can I ask you if I understand what's
> happened to you?
> CHUCK: Uh-huh.
> THERAPIST: You've been through bad trauma in the service—we
> haven't discussed the details, but it's clear you've been through hell in
> a hellish war, seeing some of your buddies die. In a place like Iraq, it's
> hard to know who or what to trust. The deployment left you feeling

numb, and then when you came home, nothing felt real or safe, either. It was hard to adjust. And you've kept reliving the war even though you're not in Iraq anymore.

CHUCK: Yes sir, that's right.

THERAPIST: So we call the symptoms you've developed PTSD. It's a treatable problem, it's not your fault, and I think we have a good chance of you getting a lot better in just these 14 weeks—we're at week 3 now. With PTSD, it's like the war's still going on: you're expecting bombs to go off in your environment, and inside you feel numb but it's like there are bombs of powerful feelings, too, that you have to ward off. Booby-traps everywhere. And feeling numb, it's hard to read the terrain, hard to adjust to being stateside again. We call the difficulty in adjustment a *role transition*. What I suggest is that we spend the remaining 11 weeks of treatment helping you decode your feelings so that you can decide whom you can trust and whom you can't. If you get more in touch with your emotions, less numb, it will be a whole lot easier to read what's going on, you should feel a lot safer, and your symptoms should fade away. Does that make sense to you?

CHUCK: Yeah. I guess. Just don't know that anything's going to be much better in any 11 weeks.

THERAPIST: That might be a happy surprise. So if it's okay, I'm just going to ask you to focus on your feelings when you're dealing with other people, to try to see what your feelings are telling you about what's going on.

They agreed to meet at a regular time each week, and that there would be no formal homework except for Chuck to pay attention to his interpersonal encounters and his feelings. With agreement on the formulation, they passed into the middle phase of treatment.

Middle Phase. The subsequent sessions dealt with affective attunement. The therapist began each session by asking how things had been since they last met. Chuck remained guarded, mostly relating dealings with his wife and kids and a lawn dispute that developed with his suburban neighbors over the placement of a fence and a fruit tree. He reported feeling numb most of the time; the world seeming detached, unreal, and trivial. Yet periodically he would get frustrated and explode: his wife and children started to give him a wide berth, which made him feel unloved. The issue of the fence seemed trivial, and yet it was a critical boundary war that reminded him of military perimeters and seemed to raise a question of safety versus danger. He was considering hiring a lawyer to sue the neighbors.

The therapist repeatedly asked in these situations: "So how do you feel when that happens?" Chuck initially answered that he didn't feel anything, just numb. He didn't know how he felt. On discussion, he began to acknowledge feeling a little something, maybe "upset."

CHUCK: So I wanted to be helpful with the kids, tried to get involved, and my wife Judy kind of froze me out, just went on without me. [Silence]

THERAPIST: So you wanted to help and it was like she didn't notice, or didn't want your help?

CHUCK: I think she noticed, but she thinks I'm a menace, doesn't trust me with the kids.

THERAPIST: Uh-uh. So what was that like for you?

CHUCK: What do you mean? I'm used to it.

THERAPIST: Did you have a feeling when you tried to help and Judy ignored you?

CHUCK: No. It's okay. . . . I guess maybe a little upset.

THERAPIST: Yeah?

CHUCK: So yeah, maybe my wife got me a little upset when she looked at me that way. All I was trying to do was help.

THERAPIST: What kind of upset? What does it feel like?

CHUCK: I don't know. Nothing. A little rise in my chest, maybe.

THERAPIST: Huh. What do you call that feeling?

CHUCK: Maybe, frustrated?

THERAPIST: Yes? Frustrated?

CHUCK: Kind of annoyed.

After sitting with this feeling for a while—not rushing to the point, but letting Chuck tolerate the emotion, letting it sink in:

THERAPIST: So you were a little annoyed, angry at Judy ignoring you. Think it was reasonable to have that feeling?

CHUCK: I don't know. I don't like getting angry.

THERAPIST: Look, it can be a problem if you express too much anger, but it's helpful to know when you feel that way. Anger tells you when someone's treated you badly, and feeling that way gives you a chance to understand the situation and respond. Again, was it reasonable for you to feel some anger in that situation?

CHUCK: I guess a little. But it reminds me of when I got lethal mad in Iraq.

THERAPIST: So, what's that mean?

CHUCK: I don't want to get like that with her.

THERAPIST: You don't want your anger to get out of control.

CHUCK: Yes, sir.

THERAPIST: But feeling angry about her behavior is reasonable? If you could find a way to express it.

CHUCK: I guess.

Having normalized the anger:

THERAPIST: So, if it's a reasonable reaction and you don't want to explode, what options do you have?

They then role-played scenarios, with the therapist taking Judy's role. Chuck wanted to trust his wife—they'd once had what felt like a good relationship— and wanted her to trust him. On the other hand, things were not going well, and both feared his "exploding." The role play allowed Chuck to practice saying what he wanted, and the tone in which he could say it. At first this came out crudely:

CHUCK: "You don't trust me as a parent. Fuck you." [Silence]

THERAPIST: How did that sound?

CHUCK: It's how I feel.

THERAPIST: Good. How did it feel to say that?

CHUCK: To the point. I guess good to get it off my chest. But also not good. She'd be hurt.

THERAPIST: Okay, well is there another way you could put it that might go over better with her?

CHUCK: "You don't trust me, and it makes me angry. I was just trying to help." [Silence]

THERAPIST: "I'm sorry, I wasn't trying to make you upset. I do trust you."

CHUCK: "No you don't. You haven't really given me a chance since I've gotten back."

THERAPIST: "I'm sorry, it's been hard for both of us. I appreciate your help, and you are their dad."

CHUCK: "Okay, then." [Silence]

THERAPIST: How did that feel?

CHUCK: Better.

THERAPIST: Good! Did you say what you wanted to say?

CHUCK: Yeah, enough.

THERAPIST: Was there something more you wanted to add?

CHUCK: No, that was the point.

THERAPIST: Great! What about the way you said it: what did you feel about your tone of voice?

CHUCK: Maybe not angry enough.

THERAPIST: Want to try it again?

They rehearsed some more.

THERAPIST: I agree that you're getting there. I noticed that you pointed out that *she made you feel angry*, that's good communication. No way to misunderstand that.

CHUCK: I guess.

THERAPIST: So, do you feel comfortable saying that to Judy? Because this kind of situation is likely to come up again.

CHUCK: Think so.

THERAPIST: Great. I know you don't like getting angry, but anger's part of life: things are going to happen, people are going to annoy you the way they annoy everyone. When they do, it's a kind of "trust moment": if you tell someone that they're bothering you, and why, one of two things can happen. Either they can apologize, and you can try to talk things out—in which case you're establishing a kind of trust, building a safe space. Or they can ignore you and keep on bothering you, in which case I guess you can't trust them. Telling them you're angry allows them to respond, and it gets the anger off your chest so you don't have to carry it around like a loaded weapon. That can feel really uncomfortable and contribute to your agitation. Also, sometimes people bother you without really meaning to, and if you don't bring it up, they're not going to know and will keep doing it.

CHUCK: Makes sense.

During a role play, when Chuck threw in: "You don't understand what I've been through!" the therapist responded, as Judy: "Well, I'd like to understand. You've never seemed to want to talk to me about it." Chuck seemed briefly taken aback, and they role-played his talking to her more.

So therapy proceeded: focusing initially on normalizing negative emotions and helping the patient name them, to build an emotional vocabulary ("What kind of 'upset'? What do you call that feeling?"). As Chuck developed that vocabulary, the focus shifted to verbalizing those feelings in interpersonal encounters, and using that emotional vocabulary to master situations. Week by week, "How have things been since we last met?" elicited tensions between the patient and his wife, kids, neighbors, and co-workers. Rather than exploding or retreating, Chuck began to try to talk his way through these encounters, and as he succeeded he began to see anger not as an enemy but an ally. He began to talk about having a pressure-relief valve through which he could blow off steam before the pressure built up.

By mid-treatment (week 7), Chuck's CAPS score had fallen from 85 to 52, a considerable improvement that still left him in the moderately severe PTSD symptom range. Nonetheless, he recognized his progress and agreed with the score. (As an engineer, he appreciated having the metric.) By this time he had pulled back from his initial urges to wreck his neighbor's yard or hire lawyers to sue. Things were still tense but markedly improved at work and home. The progress accelerated in the latter half of treatment.

Termination. Early in session 10, the therapist noted that they would be finishing in four weeks: "We can talk about that if you'd like." Chuck initially shrugged this off, but in session 11:

> CHUCK: You know, when I came here I thought I was a crazy person and you were going to treat me as a crazy person; I didn't trust you at all. This has really changed my life, saved my life maybe, and while I don't like the commute and can use the time, I'm going to miss this in some ways.

This was a striking measure of how far he'd come. At this point, Chuck and his wife were talking about feelings in a way both would have considered un-imaginable a few months before. Tension in the house had dropped. Chuck felt he was being a pretty good husband and father, where he had felt himself a dangerous failure before entering treatment. Sex with Judy was better and felt more intimate than it ever had before. He felt the kids were looking up to their hero Dad rather than fearing him. His boss spontaneously complimented Chuck on how well he was handling the adjustment post-deployment.

> THERAPIST: You were never crazy; you had PTSD, and you've really been brave in tackling it and making it better. As you said a while back, handling your strong emotions felt like defusing an IED, not easy; but you did it, and you're using them in a very impressive way. You've been brave.
>
> CHUCK: Thanks, Doc.

He was much better: by the end of 14 weeks, his CAPS score had fallen to 23, a huge improvement. He no longer met *DSM-IV* criteria for PTSD. He wasn't drinking, his depression had resolved, as had the paranoid personality dis-order symptoms so prominent at the start of treatment. Chuck felt he had a new lease on life, and that he didn't need further treatment at this point.

Treatment concluded as scheduled, with the therapist asking Chuck to check in after six months, or before if needed. Chuck gruffly hugged his therapist in departing. At six month follow-up, he reported feeling fine, had had a work promotion, and said things were "great" at home.

This is a dramatically positive story; not all cases go so smoothly. On the other hand, patients in extreme pain, once engaged, have great incentive to work on their problems. Although the therapist could conceivably have formulated the treatment as either a role dispute (particularly at home) or a role transition, or even grief over his lost buddies, the global range of Chuck's adjustment difficulties argued for focusing on this role transition. Note, too, how different the process of this IPT case was, in focusing on defining and normalizing affect and using it to win small interpersonal victories, from an exposure therapy that would have focused on past traumatic events in Fallujah.

CASE EXAMPLE 3 [TREATED BY KATHRYN BLEIBERG, PH.D.]

Deborah, a 32-year-old single white woman working in public relations with chronic PTSD and recurrent major depression, was referred by a trauma treatment clinic where she had previously received Prolonged Exposure therapy. In her initial phone call, she stated that, although she liked the therapist who provided the exposure therapy, she disliked having to describe and listen to tapes of her past traumatic memories and was interested in a psychotherapy that focused on her current problems. Her PTSD symptoms were related to sexual abuse at least several times per week from ages 7–8 by stepbrothers who were 6–7 years her senior. Her chief complaint: "I am having a lot of the symptoms I have had before, and I'm really depressed."

On SCID and CAPS interviews, Deborah met *DSM-IV* criteria for chronic PTSD. On the SCID she also met criteria for recurrent major depression, but had no history of alcohol or substance abuse or dependence. She had no personality disorder by SCID-II evaluation. For two months prior to her evaluation, Deborah reported worsening of dissociative symptoms, difficulty falling asleep, nightmares, flashbacks, intense psychological and physical distress when exposed to reminders of her abuse, increased irritability, difficulty concentrating, hypervigilance, exaggerated startle response, and depressed mood. She reported having experienced these symptoms in varying degrees since childhood and that they had intensified after visiting her family in Texas several months earlier. She reported also feeling unhappy at work, where her boss has been overly critical of her, and was in the process of looking for a new job.

Course of Treatment. At baseline, her PSS-SR score was 89, a severe score (maximum = 119). Initial sessions introduced the IPT approach, assessed symptoms, and provided psychoeducation about PTSD as well as depression. The therapist emphasized the impact of both illnesses on her social and work relationships and overall functioning. The therapist took an *interpersonal inventory* assessing current and past relationship patterns and began helping Deborah identify how her traumatic experiences and PTSD symptoms interfered with her interpersonal interactions and social and professional relationships.

Deborah's parents divorced when she was one year old, and her mother remarried when she was three. They moved around a lot with the stepfather and his sons before settling in Texas when she was a teenager. Deborah told her mother about the abuse shortly after it ended. Her mother was sympathetic and asked if she wanted to see a counselor. Deborah reported feeling angry, as she felt her mother "put it on me to take care of myself." Her mother did not tell the stepfather for another year, and the stepbrothers were never punished. At the time of the evaluation, she reported feeling angry at her mother for not standing up for her more, not insisting that the stepbrothers be punished, and for maintaining a close relationship with the stepfather. Deborah reported that she was reluctant to return to Texas for holidays or visits because she did not want to see her stepbrothers and feared that her mother would not keep them away from the house. She had no communication with the stepbrothers on her own.

Her biological father, described as verbally abusive, she currently spoke to once a year. She had lived with her father for about a year in her early teens, but he was verbally abusive and intrusive, often opening her mail. She felt upset with her mother for sending her to live with someone who her mother knew could harm her.

Deborah reported that growing up she "couldn't make friends." She "had difficulty fitting in." Her mother moved her around a lot, so she had to switch schools sometimes in mid-semester. She reported having attended a large, liberal arts college where she began forming female friendships that she had since maintained. She stated she was heterosexual, yet had no romantic relationships with men. She felt nervous around guys and formed a reputation in college for being "cold and uninterested" in dating. After graduation, she moved to New York City and began working in public relations. She reported that her boss had been overly critical of her work and told Deborah that she was "rude and condescending." She wanted to leave the job and had been looking at positions elsewhere. Deborah reported feeling uncomfortable with people she did not know and socially awkward at parties. She would occasionally go out with a colleague from work, but said her closest friends, from college, lived outside New York. She reported feeling easily angered but that she couldn't express her anger directly. She would instead act irritable and complain to third parties about how she felt. She avoided crowds and crowded subways for fear of men getting too close to her. She reported that she used to enjoy dance classes and cooking but had not been participating in pleasurable activities in the few months prior to her evaluation.

The therapist gave Deborah *the sick role*, explaining that she suffered from PTSD and depression, and provided psychoeducation about their symptoms. The therapist emphasized that these illnesses were not her fault, and were treatable. In addition, the therapist gave her copies of pages describing PTSD and depression from *DSM-IV*. In the following session, Deborah expressed with relief that, until that discussion and reading about PTSD, she had thought her symptoms were "just weird about me—now I realize I have symptoms—there is an explanation." The therapist linked the recrudescence of Deborah's symptoms to her conflicts with her mother and unhappiness at work, framing the *problem areas and focus of treatment* as a role dispute—her ongoing conflict with her mother; and a role transition—her search for a new job. The patient accepted these foci.

The middle sessions explored the potential for improving Deborah's relationship with her mother, addressing her conflicts with her boss, and pursuing a new job. Working from recent and anticipated interactions, therapist and patient *explored how the patient felt in those situations*, naming and validating her feelings. They then considered what *options* she had for handling these situations. Initially tentative, the patient was able to suggest feasible options with the therapist's encouragement. Next, they *role-played* different options for communicating her needs to her mother, as well as to work colleagues and peers. They also role-played phone conversations inquiring about job opportunities and responding to questions in job interviews. Addressing the patient's current life situations, the therapist helped her better understand her feelings and needs and express them to others, as well as present herself more effectively on job interviews.

The therapist continually related Deborah's currently feeling vulnerable, mistrusting others, withdrawing from others, and excessive anger reactions to having been traumatized: "These are part of PTSD." At the same time, the therapist empathized with Deborah's understandable need to protect herself against being vulnerable to others. She related Deborah's difficulty in prioritizing and asserting her needs, and her negative self-image, to PTSD and depression. Like many who have been abused, Deborah perceived herself as damaged and feared that others would be see her as damaged or deduce that she had been abused. The therapist related this misperception to having been traumatized—PTSD—and reminded her that abuse, while part of her life experience, did not have to define her.

In addition to working on the focal problem areas, the therapist encouraged Deborah to work on current relationships and forming new ones, at the same time empathizing with her fears of getting hurt and rejected. The therapist encouraged her to engage in activities that she had once enjoyed. By the end of the week 7, her PSS-SR score had fallen to 55, a clinically meaningful improvement.

One crucial moment in the therapy came after therapist and patient discussed Deborah's anger at her boss for his extremely harsh behavior toward her. The therapist validated the patient's tentative expression of angry feelings in the session: "Anyone would feel angry being treated that way." The therapist *normalized* Deborah's reaction. As she became more confident in her reaction to this mistreatment, the patient decided to lodge a complaint with the human resources department of her company. Her boss backed off and apologized, life at work became much less threatening, and Deborah felt better. She continued to look into alternative job options and to polish her interviewing in sessions.

The other important theme concerned her relationship with her mother. Deborah described feeling angry at her mom for not protecting her from her stepbrothers or ensuring they were punished for molesting her, yet reported feeling guilty for feeling angry, as she saw her mother as fragile and in a difficult position. The therapist validated the patient's anger at her mother and related the excessive guilt to depression. The therapist and Deborah role-played expressing Deborah's wish that her mom be more supportive by asking the stepbrothers to stay away from the house when she visits. She then was better able to communicate her needs more directly to her mother. Her mother sympathized with her feelings but replied that she could not talk about the past further. The mother stated that she would try but could not promise to keep the stepsons out of the house. In a subsequent session, the therapist validated the patient's wish that her mother be more supportive, as well her disappointment that her mother continued to provide less support than she wanted. The final sessions explored whether there was an impasse in Deborah's relationship with her mother, and what the patient's further options were for dealing with it. Therapist and patient also reviewed the patient's gains in the treatment, her better handling of social interactions, and the consequent improvement in her symptoms and overall wellbeing.

At the end of treatment, Deborah felt more accepting of her mother's limitations and was able to speak to her with less distress. She felt more capable in dealing with her boss and more confident on job interviews. She reported improved relationships with her peers, was socializing more and had resumed activities such as dancing. Furthermore, she mentioned that she was no longer getting off crowded trains before her stop.

By her final, week 14 session, Deborah's PSS-SR score had fallen to 6, an essentially asymptomatic status. At six month follow-up, her PSS-SR score was 15, reflecting maintenance of her acute symptomatic improvement.

This case used two interpersonal foci, a role transition and a role dispute, situations that commonly co-occur. It would probably have been possible to cover much of the same ground in treatment under a single focus. Regardless, the patient clearly benefitted from this approach.

Role transitions can take many forms, depending in part on the patient's history and the nature of the abuse they suffer. The above examples hopefully illustrate the IPT approach to treating patients with PTSD: the focus is on the patient's improving the patient's affective awareness and current interpersonal functioning rather than on reconstructing the trauma and exposure to trauma reminders.

8

IPT for PTSD—Grief

"Give sorrow words. The grief that does not speak
Whispers the o'erfraught heart and bids it break."
                                        —SHAKESPEARE, *Macbeth, IV, 3 (1606)*

Grief—complicated bereavement—follows the death of a significant other, the loss of a key relationship in an individual's life. The death of a close family member has long been known to rank among the most stressful of life events (Holmes & Rahe, 1967). Grief might become the focus of treatment if a patient developed PTSD after having witnessed the violent death or murder of a spouse, child, other family member, or close friend. In our randomized trial, six (16%) of 38 patients who began IPT focused on grief.

CASE EXAMPLE

Leonard, a 65-year-old married white businessman, presented in 2006 for treatment of PTSD that began following the World Trade Center attack of September 11, 2001. Living in Hoboken, New Jersey, almost with a view of the World Trade Center, Leonard knew that his eldest son Rob, 35, was working on the upper floors of the North Tower. Hearing the news, he ran out of his house and found a high vantage point from whence he helplessly watched the burning buildings while listening on a Walkman to news reports. Following the collapse of the Towers, he watched innumerable repetitions on television. Subsequently, even when he had stopped watching TV, scenes of the terrorist attack replayed in his mind, as did images of his lost son.

He developed agitation, anhedonia, insomnia, and distractibility. He stopped eating and lost 45 pounds over several years. He withdrew from others, stopped leaving the house, and sat alone in his room. Although he had three other grown children, who with his wife apparently did their best to comfort him, he felt he had lost his golden child and life no longer had meaning. He wished that he could die himself, that he had died in place of his son, that he had died before he ever saw such a day. His wife Rose arranged for him to come to treatment, which he approached reluctantly and hopelessly. On presentation in mid-2006, he met *DSM-IV* criteria for both PTSD and major depression, with a CAPS score of 68 (severe) and Ham-D score of 30 (severe). Leonard followed his wife and eldest daughter into the office with downcast eyes.

Leonard was a tall, graying, formerly athletic but now too thin white man, appearing older than his stated age, showing several days' growth of beard. He was adequately groomed, casually dressed in jeans and a plaid work shirt. His movements were mildly agitated, his speech soft and restricted but fluent, and he looked at the floor more than at the therapist. His mood was anxious and depressed, with a constricted, sometimes detached affect. Thinking was marked by ruminations about his cursed life and lost son. There was no suggestion of psychotic symptoms. He reported passive suicidal ideation without formal plans or intent. His intelligence appeared above average, his insight limited (he did not see himself as having a psychiatric condition, just that his world had ended). Sensorium was clear.

The therapist spoke briefly to the wife and daughter in Leonard's presence but, gauging that the patient would be able to provide a history on his own, asked them to wait outside the office. He then introduced himself to Leonard:

THERAPIST: You look like you've been through something. How can I help you?

LEONARD: I don't think anyone can help me. My boy Rob was killed on 9/11, and my life is over too.

THERAPIST: I'm so sorry to hear that. What a terrible thing! Tell me about Rob.

LEONARD: He was great. He worked at [a financial firm] on the 104th floor of the North Tower. He was a superstar, had his whole life ahead of him. . . . And now he's dead.

This was trauma history enough. Although Leonard returned from time to time to ruminations about the World Trade Center, the rest of his treatment focused on grief, following the usual IPT approach. The therapist asked about what Leonard's relationship with Rob had been like, starting with the positive; and what he missed about him. As treatment progressed, they also addressed rough points in the relationship, difficult times, things that hadn't been so wonderful. But the focus stayed on the relationship and the son, not on the trauma that had separated them.

The therapist expressed sympathy and began to take a history, starting with Leonard's relationship with Rob and extending to the more general family situation. Len had been married for 38 years to Rose, and Rob had been his eldest of three sons and a daughter. Leonard loved his wife and other children, but said Rob had always been his favorite, the one he drilled to competitively "follow in my footsteps" as both a high school and college athlete and a subsequent business success. Rob had been highly successful working in mergers and acquisitions, had married, had had two young children, and had lived in Manhattan, not far from his parents across the Hudson River. Leonard had frequently taken the ferry from Hoboken to visit this favored branch of the family. Now he never came to Manhattan at all.

An interpersonal inventory revealed that Leonard had always seen himself as a family man, the patriarch who barbecued on the Fourth of July. He had a few business colleagues he golfed with, but no one he confided in. Indeed, he had long prided himself on his self-sufficiency, on his capacity to control his feelings without needing to burden others.

Leonard denied prior trauma, mood or anxiety disorders, suicidality, and prior psychiatric treatment. He reported drinking two or three scotches a night, without evident adverse effects; he denied other drug use. His medical history was notable for smoking a pack of cigarettes daily for 40 years; no thyroid history or physical trauma. He had been taking a diuretic for hypertension for fifteen years.

Toward the end of the first session, the therapist pointed out that while alcohol might help Leonard fall asleep, it might also worsen his insomnia and risked compounding his depression. The therapist suggested cutting back, at least until Leonard got his symptoms under control.

Notice that, from the start of this opening session, the therapist focused history-taking on the patient's relationship with the deceased son, not on the trauma *per se*. This set the tone for IPT. At the end of the second session of a planned 14-week treatment, the therapist provided a formulation:

THERAPIST: You've given me a lot of helpful background; will you tell me whether I understand everything you've told me? You seem to have had a successful and happy life until you reached 60 and your son was killed. You have always been able to take care of yourself and control your life and protect your family; but who could have imagined an event like this? Losing a son, and maybe especially your favorite, eldest son, is one of the worst traumas anyone can undergo. Like many people who were directly affected by the

World Trade Center attack, you've developed posttraumatic stress disorder—as I told you, your score on the CAPS scale is in the severe range. PTSD is a treatable condition, and it's not your fault. The same is true for the depression that often accompanies PTSD. It's all a kind of *complicated grief.* You've been struggling to keep your feelings in, but it might really help for us to talk more about Rob, what you miss about him and your lost close relationship with him. If you can process those feelings, you're likely to feel a lot better. I'm confident that we can get you feeling better in the remaining 12 weeks of this treatment.

Leonard was not pleased about being in therapy, which he saw as a weakness. But, he sighed, "I don't really have a choice, I don't have much more to lose." So he persevered.

The therapist formally gave him the *sick role*, noting that this capable man would not be functioning at his best under the severe symptom load he was carrying. He encouraged Leonard to "do the best you can, but give yourself a break if you can't function at your peak," until his symptoms began to recede. They planned regular weekly 50-minute sessions.

The middle phase of therapy focused on Leonard's feelings. He brought in photographs of Rob that helped him break through his numbness and dissolve into tears.

LEONARD: Sorry. I shouldn't cry.
THERAPIST: Why not? Aren't you discussing something extremely sad?
LEONARD: I don't want to burden you, to mess up your office with Kleenex.
THERAPIST: It's not a burden. Your talking about your feelings helps me understand where you are. It's natural to have such feelings when you've lost a child.

Although the session focused on a discussion of Leonard's generally close and positive relationship with Rob, it also touched on Leonard's attempts at self-containment so as not to burden his other family members.

THERAPIST: Why would you be burdening them?
LEONARD: I don't like to upset my family; I'm supposed to take care of them. And they'd think I'm weak. And they wouldn't understand.
THERAPIST: Your family wouldn't understand why you're so sad about Rob's death? . . . And do you think they don't know that [you're sad], even if you're not talking about it?

This led to an exploration of Leonard's options in communicating with his family, and a brief role play about how he might raise the topic.

The early sessions were affectively laden and increasingly powerful. Leonard tended to bring up situations rather than his feeling states. The therapist would then ask, "And how did you feel in that situation?" The therapist tried to prime the emotional pump, getting Leonard to focus on his feelings and then letting him run, taking care not to interrupt. It took a little while for this to develop: at first Leonard would complain of feeling numb, would stop talking or change the subject, clearly wary of becoming overwhelmed by his feeling states. The therapist would then step in, reassuring him ("Feelings are powerful, but they're not dangerous . . . the greater danger may lie in keeping them in"), emphasizing that IPT sessions were safe places to explore his feelings, and that the emotions might actually prove helpful in decoding his current life circumstances. Leonard sometimes began to sweat, and at the end of one early session commented on how exhausting the process felt. But he opened up more each week, and his emotions became clearer, better defined, and seemingly more controllable in his own mind as he decompressed. He began to see that the process was helping him feel better, and that the feelings actually were useful rather than dangerous.

The week 5 session continued to focus on Leonard's increasingly unguarded feelings about his son, including some mention of tensions that had arisen between them over career choices—whether or not Rob should go to business or law school. The following week, Leonard appeared considerably brighter, his posture no longer slumped, his movements far less agitated.

THERAPIST: How have things been since we last met?

LEONARD: A lot better—a lot's happened. After what we've been talking about, I decided to take the plunge: went home, pulled Rose aside and told her about how Rob's death hurts. It's not like I hadn't tried to tell her before, but this was more—detailed. I guess much more how I really felt. And I even cried in front of her. She looked a little nervous at first, because I don't think she'd ever seen me like that, but she was okay with it, and she cried, too.

THERAPIST: Wow. You really have done a lot. So what did all that feel like?

LEONARD: Good, actually. I felt closer to Rose than in a long time. I've been feeling cut off. . . ..

Toward the end of the session, they discussed activities Leonard might want to resume as ways of enjoying himself and rebuilding social supports: for example, playing golf.

The following week, his CAPS score had dropped to 39 and his Ham-D score to 18, both substantial improvements. They continued to talk about Rob, about the fact that he could have mixed feelings, positive and negative, about Rob and about his past relationship with Rob. Leonard mentioned spending more time with his wife and seeing more of his other children, feeling closer and more open with them. He had resumed golf with his business friends and was feeling better at work, if still having trouble concentrating at times.

Week 8:

THERAPIST: How have you been since we last met?

LEONARD: I guess I'm on a roll. I've been thinking about Rob, of course. The day after our last meeting, I told Rose that we had to go to Ground Zero. We had stayed away, as you know. She was a little worried about me, I think thought I'd gone nuts. "Are you sure that's a wise thing?" she wanted to know. But we took the ferry, then got a cab downtown. It freaked me out a little, but I also wanted to see where Rob had died, and going there wasn't nearly as bad as I would have thought, if I had thought about it at all.

THERAPIST: So it sounds like the PTSD isn't getting in your way the way it was. So tell me, what did going there bring up about your relationship with Rob?

Note that the IPT therapist never formally assigned homework, but simply discussing options for communicating his feelings with his family encouraged Leonard to do so. The decision to approach the site of his son's death was entirely Leonard's, not previously planned or even discussed in therapy. The IPT therapist encourages the patient to take the initiative, expressing confidence in the patient's underlying competence even at the nadir of severe PTSD. Leonard had clearly been a capable, driven man before this episode, and with a little encouragement, he took charge himself. (This helps the patient feel competent in a way he might not have had the therapist spelled everything out for him and given him an assignment.)

Subsequent sessions flew by. September 11 approached, a day Leonard had been avoiding. This year, without therapist prompting, he made a point of attending the 9/11 memorial services in the company of his surviving family members and friends. He cried openly, and reported feeling proud to do so; he also noticed that he was not alone in shedding tears, and began to see expressing his emotions as a strength rather than a weakness. By the end of therapy, he had decided to volunteer as a guide at the 9/11 site. He saw this as a way of paying tribute to his son and helping other people who had suffered from the attack.

LEONARD: I feel sad, but not depressed. And I feel good that I can show my mourning like this, maybe doing a little good.

THERAPIST: What a wonderful way to find the silver lining in this cloud of tragedy! You've really turned yourself around, and you're doing good for yourself and for others. No wonder you feel good as well as sad.

At termination, Leonard's CAPS score was 14 and his Hamilton Depression score 4, both indicating remission. He thanked the therapist and did not feel he needed more treatment: "I made my breakthrough." A year later, Leonard reported that he was nearing retirement from work but more involved in 9/11 charitable activities. He was still sad about Rob, but spending time with Rob's widowed wife and his grandchildren. He remained essentially asymptomatic.

In IPT for major depression, treating the problem area of grief routinely involves asking about how the patient learned of the deceased's death: where they were, what happened; anything proximal to the death about which—either by omission or commission—the patient might feel guilty. In our PTSD treatment study, we scrupulously avoided exploring this area in order to ensure that IPT did not address the traumatic event itself: we did not want to be accused of exposing the patient to traumatic memories. Having proved the point with that research that IPT could benefit PTSD patients without exposing patients to trauma reminders, I now have a suggestion for clinicians in treating traumatic grief: Do what feels appropriate. It wouldn't hurt to explore patient reactions to the events of the death, at least briefly. If I were treating Leonard today, I might explore further than I did then his feelings about going to the World Trade Center. IPT for grief-related PTSD, however, should still focus on the lost person and on the patient's larger relationship with the deceased, positive and negative; not principally on the traumatic death that ended it.

9

IPT for PTSD—Role Disputes

"What we've got here is failure to communicate."
—COOL HAND LUKE (1967)

Role disputes related to PTSD may present in several fashions. They might relate to the trauma: for example, a woman or man presenting for treatment might still be in an abusive relationship, unable to fend off the abuse. Alternatively, and perhaps more commonly, we see patients who have suffered prior abuse, often in childhood, and have developed PTSD. They describe current relationships in which they struggle to assert themselves, to tolerate or express their anger, or otherwise feel unsafe and overwhelmed. The task of IPT is then to help them to tolerate and understand their feelings and to use them to renegotiate their relationships, thereby relieving PTSD symptoms. Role disputes generally elicit emotionally intense sessions, provoked by the immediacy of interpersonal conflict. In our randomized trial, two (5%) of 38 patients who began IPT treatment focused on role disputes; an additional four therapies treated role disputes as a secondary focus.

CASE EXAMPLE 1

Alicia was a 43-year-old, married, white, Jewish, successful local politician and mother of two daughters whose husband, Dave, insisted on her seeking care under threat of divorce. She, bewildered, was essentially dragged into the office by her spouse, who said, "About once a month, maybe it's her period, she explodes! She needs help. I can't take this anymore." Alicia was initially a reluctant patient but felt that divorce might ruin her political career, and conceded that there were problems in their 20-year marriage.

Alicia initially said that things were okay at home, but that every so often she would "go off" in a way that she was largely unaware of until it had ended. Her husband and young children feared these angry outbursts, and although she felt guilty afterwards, she never really knew what to say, feeling that she had been pretty much absent at the time. In a detached manner, she said, "I feel bad that I upset them, but I don't really know what's going on."

On mental status examination, Alicia was an alert, attractive, expensively dressed, very well-groomed woman, perhaps with a hint too much makeup, appearing roughly her stated age. She had controlled normal movements, fluent unpressured deliberate speech, and made good eye contact. Her mood was anxious, not grossly depressed, with a controlled, superficial, nonlabile, and somewhat detached affect. She had the air of a politician: polished, slightly self-promoting, veneered, conscious of the impression she was making. Thinking was goal-directed if somewhat concrete; and she seemed careful in choosing her words. She denied suicidal and homicidal ideation and psychotic symptoms. Insight was limited: she conceded that there were problems at home, but she hardly understood why. Sensorium was clear.

On questioning, Alicia reported recurrent nightmares, which awakened her most nights: something maybe about her childhood, although she could never recall the content—and didn't really want to know. She had frequent insomnia. Her daytime concentration varied, although she wasn't sure what distracted her. She acknowledged feeling detached from her feelings, almost like she was watching herself go through life. She alluded to a difficult childhood, in which "my mother was tough sometimes, hard on me," but revealed no actual content and claimed not to remember much before the age of 15, when she left home for boarding school. Her father was a businessman, often absent from the house and evidently unengaged and passive when he was home.

Alicia met *DSM-IV* criteria for PTSD and had a Clinician-Administered PTSD Scale (CAPS) score at presentation of 55, consistent with moderately severe PTSD. Her medical and neurological history was unremarkable. She denied head trauma and seizures, as well as dysmenorrhea and premenstrual dysphoric disorder: her episodes of anger bore no temporal relationship to her menstrual cycle. She had no history of prior psychiatric treatment.

In taking a fuller history, the therapist learned that although Alicia had been a model child, "a good girl" honors student, her mother frequently punished her for minor or imagined infractions by confining her to her room for days, grounding her, and sometimes hitting her when the mother had had too much to drink.

THERAPIST: Did you ever end up in the hospital after your mother hit you?

ALICIA: No. Well, two times, but it was nothing much. One minor
fracture.

The hospital doctors had evidently not asked many questions because her
mother was "a respectable woman." Alicia said she admired her parents, who
were good providers, but tried not to get angry the way her mother did. "She
could be scary," she conceded. Alicia took pride in her ability to deflect contro-
versial media questions in her political life.

She acknowledged, however, that her husband had a point about her behavior. Most of the time Alicia was pleasant, efficient, and in control. Every
now and then, perhaps once a month, she would unexpectedly "see red" about
something at home: her two generally well-behaved children's behavior, or
something her husband said or did, or maybe even nothing that she could put
her finger on. She had difficulty describing what happened, providing vague,
dissociated memories of these incidents, but she knew they generally ended
with the whole family upset, even seeming afraid of her. Her husband said she
shrieked and occasionally threw things, although she had never hit anyone.
Alicia, meanwhile, felt guilty for having lost control and frightened her family,
and swore each time that she would handle herself better, that this incident
would be the last. Her insight into what actually occurred at these times was
surprisingly limited, but she perceived her emotional state as something that
required careful control.

The therapist asked her to recall the last such event, the one that had precipitated her coming for treatment.

ALICIA: I don't even know. I think I had made dinner, but my husband
was futzing around with his computer, and Joanie was in the
bathroom, so I was at the table with just Clara sitting there, and the
food was getting cold. And then I saw red, I guess. The next thing
I know, the kids are crying in their rooms, my husband has locked
himself up in the study, and no one had dinner.

THERAPIST: So what happened?

ALICIA: You know, I must've said something to get everyone upset.
[Silence]

THERAPIST: [after a pause] Like, what might you have said?

ALICIA: I don't know, something. [Silence] . . . Like maybe something
about them being ungrateful.

THERAPIST: You mean, for dinner?

ALICIA: Yes. I mean, I work, I pick up the kids from school, I make
dinner, and they don't even come to the table. I'm only one person. So
probably something about that.

THERAPIST: So how were you feeling when you said something?

ALICIA: [Pausing, embarrassed. In a quiet voice] Like they should have been there. At the table. Like, what's their problem?

THERAPIST: So what do you call that emotion, about "they should-have-been-there-but-they-weren't"?

ALICIA: They weren't appreciating what I do.

THERAPIST: Right. So what's your feeling about their not appreciating you?

ALICIA: I don't know what to call that. Upset.

THERAPIST: What kind of upset? What would you call that?

ALICIA: Like, a little . . . frustrated?

THERAPIST: Frustrated, like annoyed, angry?

ALICIA: I guess, but also that they didn't care about me the way they should. "Angry" sounds bad—I don't want to be angry, they are my family.

THERAPIST: Frustrated?

ALICIA: A little. Or as you said, annoyed.

THERAPIST: Aha. And unappreciated—you felt a little hurt?

ALICIA: Maybe, I don't know. But I don't see why you're making such a thing about this.

THERAPIST: The kinds of feelings you have may have something to do with your getting upset at your family. . ... Do you think you might have had reason to feel a little frustrated and hurt?

ALICIA: No. Yes. Yes, I guess a little. But it's only a meal, it shouldn't turn into World War III!

THERAPIST: But we're touching on something important here. So you came home, having worked a full day, made dinner, and your husband and daughter don't show up, and you feel something. And the next thing you know, it's World War III, although it sounds like you're foggy on the details?

ALICIA: Yes, that's right.

THERAPIST: So you felt . . . frustration and hurt?

ALICIA: A little, but I wasn't really thinking that at the time, and it's really not such a big deal, a few minutes late to dinner.

Although Alicia had (mostly covert) disagreements with several members of her family, and with her office staff, the main difficulties and the imminent crisis lay in her marriage. The couple had met late in college, had fallen in love and admired one another, but had always had a certain interpersonal distance. Alicia wanted Dave to see her as an impressive person, although she didn't always (or even often) feel that way. A quality she felt made her impressive was her self-control. Alicia had difficulty talking to him—as to everyone—about her childhood and about her inner feelings. Dave had initially been an occasional sounding board for her frustrations. But as years passed and pressures mounted in their careers and in their childcare responsibilities, she had ceased to confide in him. They worked well together at dinner parties, on election platforms, and in other public settings. Their private life, however, had atrophied. Their once robust sex life had faded. They tried to focus on their children, and while they generally were polite to one another, they were increasingly distant. He periodically got angry at her and accused her of being an "empty politico," which hurt her feelings. She tended not to respond to such outbursts. When Dave complained that she didn't really love him, she would reply in a strained voice, "Of course I love you"—yet kept her distance. She felt bewildered and betrayed: that Dave did not understand her, rejected her emotionally and sexually.

THERAPIST: So how do you feel about your husband?

ALICIA: He's a good man. Maybe he has reason to be fed up with me.

THERAPIST: Those aren't really feelings, though. What emotions do you have?

ALICIA: I love him. I guess I'm worried he may give up on me or see me as a loser. Maybe he's right that I'm an "empty politico"?

THERAPIST: Do you trust him?

ALICIA: Trust? I don't think I really trust anyone.

The therapist offered a formulation:

THERAPIST: We've established that you are suffering from PTSD, with a high score on the CAPS scale. The PTSD seems to have begun with physical and emotional abuse by your mother as you were growing up. ...

ALICIA: Abuse! I don't know. That seems too strong. It makes me uncomfortable when you say that.

THERAPIST: I don't mean to make you uncomfortable, and it's good you can tell me that. Look, if you ended up in the hospital with a fracture, that technically meets the state's criteria for abuse. And the general atmosphere of fear in which you grew up seems the best explanation for your PTSD symptoms.

ALICIA: Just don't call it abuse. I hate to think about my mother that way. [Shudders]

THERAPIST: We're not going to focus on what happened back then, but on the effects of PTSD on your current life. One of the consequences of PTSD is often feeling numb, not being aware of your feelings, which is what you've described.

ALICIA: Uh-huh.

THERAPIST: And if you're numb, it's hard to read your feelings in situations, you know?

ALICIA: I usually don't feel much of anything. I just want things to go smoothly. Try to stay in control.

THERAPIST: But those feelings, even the uncomfortable ones, like anger, can help you read what's happening in relationships and help you figure out how to handle them. If you're having trouble reading your relationships because of PTSD, they often go wrong. So one consequence of PTSD for you seems to be that you're in a struggle with Dave, a struggle that we call a *role dispute*. As your husband, Dave could be providing you important support in your life, but you seem to feel distanced, at odds with him. I suggest that we spend the remaining 12 weeks of treatment focusing on your marriage, figuring out where you and Dave are having difficulty and how you can fix it. If we do this, there's a good chance that you can improve the relationship, and your PTSD symptoms should follow. Does that make sense to you?

ALICIA: Yes, that sounds like a plan. Although I doubt I can really change our marriage in that short a time.

A pattern developed in the early weeks of therapy. Alicia characteristically responded to the opening question ("How've things been since we last met?") by describing an incident rather than a mood state. On exploring the incident, she would initially deny having any feelings, but on discussion acknowledged some, hesitantly at first. As this pattern continued, she became better able to name the feelings: "frustration" and "annoyance" became acceptably translated to "anger," although she had initially dismissed that term as a characteristic of her mother that she did not want to emulate.

THERAPIST: But everyone gets angry. It just means that someone's bothering you or doing something you don't like. It's not a bad feeling, it just tells you about someone's bad behavior. It's normal to get angry; it is a social signal that tells you something important. If you ignore it, the problem is likely to persist. If you can find a way to express it more comfortably, perhaps it won't build up into one of the explosions you've described.

The therapist continued to elicit and normalize her feelings, particularly the negative affects. Alicia said she was "allergic" to anger and sadness. She joked that these were not "politically correct" emotions. But over time she increasingly relaxed and accepted her feelings. As she remained very concerned about their expression—most concerned about expressing anger—she and the therapist role-played interactions. The IPT message is that emotions are useful social signals.

Session 5:

ALICIA: So my aide hadn't prepared the report I wanted, and I guess you'd want me to say I was annoyed.

THERAPIST: I'm not trying to manipulate you. What you feel is what you feel. How did you feel?

ALICIA: I guess I was angry that she had two weeks to get a few pages ready and couldn't do it. Did a terrible job. I'd never be that inefficient.

THERAPIST: Were there any extenuating circumstances? Did your aide have other pressures that might have distracted her?

ALICIA: No, I made it clear this was the number one priority. And it isn't the first time this has happened. She's unreliable.

THERAPIST: And what's your feeling, about her being unreliable?

ALICIA: Annoy—well, anger.

THERAPIST: And is it reasonable to feel angry if she's unreliable with an important assignment?

ALICIA: Yes, I think so. Although you know I don't like that.

THERAPIST: How have you handled that with Sally [the aide] in the past?

ALICIA: I've just let it go. [Pause]

THERAPIST: Oh?

ALICIA: Well, you know. I don't like confrontations.

THERAPIST: So are you angry not only about this report, but about past things you've asked her to do?

ALICIA: Yes.

THERAPIST: Think it's reasonable to be a little angry at this point?

ALICIA: Yes, although it's not my thing.

THERAPIST: So what can you do?

ALICIA: I could not entrust her with priorities anymore. Or I guess I could tell her I don't need her services.

THERAPIST: Yes, those are options. Is she just not worth keeping on staff?

ALICIA: [Reflecting] Sally does have some good qualities, just maybe not with time management and thoroughness. She has good ideas, like in my last campaign. She can be compassionate.

THERAPIST: So before you give up or fire her, is there something else you could do?

ALICIA: Like what?

THERAPIST: What are your options?

ALICIA: I guess I could say something. . . .

This dialogue led to a productive series of role plays in which Alicia tried saying different things, ranging between too indirect and too confrontational ("Where was that page I was looking for?" vs. "I'm sick of your not getting anything done!"); in question form at first ("Sally, where was that page?"); later, with therapist encouragement ("I notice you're asking her a question. Is it a question, or is there a declarative statement you'd like to make?"), as a declarative statement ("I need to talk to you about how I'm feeling about things. I feel like I give you important things to do because I rely on you, and then you let me down.") They also discussed and practiced modulating her tone of voice, so that it was neither too weak nor too strong.

This discussion in the sessions addressed a difficult relationship outside the home rather than the marital dispute on which the treatment had generally focused. Nonetheless, once Alicia had brought up her problem with Sally, it seemed to the therapist an important parallel instance in which Alicia could understand her feelings and modulate their expression in a constructive way. Working with this material validated Alicia's raising it in session, and certainly maintained the same theme of her irritation in interpersonal disputes. Focusing on work also seemed to be a "safer" place for Alicia to test her feelings than in the more charged atmosphere of her marriage. This had not been part of the therapist's plan, but appeared a reasonable adjustment in the face of the patient's presentation of material.

Session 7 began with the therapist asking, "How have things been since we last met?" Alicia, looking brighter and calmer, responded that she had set up a time to talk with Sally and had talked to her, reasonably calmly and assertively. Sally had made excuses, then burst into tears and apologized, saying she how much she admired Alicia and wanted to help her work. Alicia reported that she had felt a little frightened by Sally's crying, but had felt gratified by the way the encounter proceeded. Moreover, Sally had since been more efficient and reliable. The therapist explored how Alicia had felt during the encounter.

ALICIA: Nervous at first, then really relieved, and really good. By the time we stopped and she went back to her desk, I felt much more in control of the situation.

THERAPIST: That's great! And how've you been feeling since?

ALICIA: A lot better, more relaxed. Though it took something out of me.

THERAPIST: That's wonderful. So this is what we've been talking
    about: you risked bringing up your feelings, Sally was able to hear
    them, and the relationship between you feels better. And you feel
    better.

ALICIA: Yes, it's true.

THERAPIST: Terrific! And if you can do that with Sally, perhaps the
    same approach will also work with Dave?

ALICIA: Dave? Yes, it's worth a try.

Thus emboldened (if still cautious), Alicia talked more about tensions in
their relationship. She felt unsupported and rejected by Dave—now that she
thought about it, angry at him. Although they maintained a façade of normalcy in public and with their children, they barely spoke and had little physical contact.

ALICIA: I'm hurt and angry. He doesn't seem to care about me; he just
    goes through the motions.

THERAPIST: Does he know you feel that way?

ALICIA: Of course.

THERAPIST: You've told him?

ALICIA: Not in so many words. But he must know from the way
    I behave toward him. He must sense it from the way I look at him
    at times.

THERAPIST: How is that?

ALICIA: I don't know. He should just see it.

THERAPIST: How would you like him to show that he cares?

ALICIA: I'd like him to take me in his arms and tell me so. But that's not
    his style, at least not these days.

THERAPIST: You'd like him to hold you and tell you.

ALICIA: Yes. Yes!

THERAPIST: Are those reasonable feelings for you to have?

ALICIA: Yes, I think so.

THERAPIST: Okay. I think so, too. Are you sure he knows that you want
    him to behave like that?

ALICIA: He should. He has to.

THERAPIST: What options do you have to let him know?

ALICIA: I guess, like with Sally, I could tell him. But I shouldn't have to.

THERAPIST: It would be nicer if he could do it spontaneously. But from
    what you've said, it's been a while. So how might you communicate
    what you'd like?

ALICIA: I could say—Dave, I need to talk to you about how I'm feeling about things . . . [tails off]

THERAPIST: [Waiting a beat.] Uh-huh?

ALICIA: I feel like we've been having problems in our marriage, and I want it to get better. I feel hurt and frustrated by the distance between us. It's probably my fault, and I know you think I'm an empty politico, but. . ..

THERAPIST: Yes?

ALICIA: I love you, and I want you to take me in your arms and tell me you care. —Oh, that sounds so corny!

THERAPIST: You think so? I thought that was really sincere and caring. But how would you want to change that?

They tried a few other approaches.

Session 8 brought no real developments. Alicia had thought about talking to her husband, but hadn't gotten around to it—she conceded she was frightened. She and her therapist spent the session exploring her feelings and doing more role plays, including playing out contingencies: how could she handle things if Dave avoided a conversation, or dismissed her, or got annoyed? They ended up talking about "going through the emotions" in the marriage as opposed to "going through the motions."

Session 9, for which the therapist had had high hopes of Alicia confronting Dave with her feelings, again passed relatively uneventfully. Alicia talked about her office, where Sally was doing a better job, and about her relationships with her children, which also seemed to be deepening and improving. She and Dave had not had sex in a few months, though, and she expressed frustration about that. Her therapist asked: "What options do you have to deal with that?"

Session 10:

ALICIA: You always ask me, "How have things been since we last met?" I'm going to beat you to the punch. Things have been, as you would say, really interesting. I took the plunge and talked to him—and it went well!

THERAPIST: Great! Tell me!

ALICIA: Well, I told him at dinner that we needed to talk that night, and he looked puzzled, a little nervous, but he said okay. So after we got the girls put down for the night, I opened a bottle of white wine and we talked. I tried the lines we'd practiced, and it wasn't completely smooth, but it was pretty good. I told him I loved him and felt hurt and frustrated and all that. That I felt he had given up on me, even on making love, and that it was really frustrating. And when I got to the part about wanting him to hold me—he did! And we made love for the first time in forever, and it felt a little awkward at first, but then much closer than maybe it ever had. I was nervous, but I also feel more like I can trust him. It's like everything we've been talking about all this time came together at once.

THERAPIST: Amazing. You did a great job! How are you feeling?

ALICIA: I feel so much better. The next morning I was a little worried, like would it last? And that night, I got nervous, because Dave said *he* wanted to have a talk with *me*. So I was sure for a moment that it was all over. But then what he wanted to talk about was how I would blow up, see red. He had noticed that it hadn't been happening for some weeks, but he said that was what really hurt our relationship, my explosions.

THERAPIST: [looks expectantly]

ALICIA: Well, so first I wasn't sure what to say. I guess I stiffened up, because he looked tense. But I guess I thought about what we'd been talking about here, and so. . . I told him that I had trouble with anger because of PTSD, but that I was trying to express my feelings more directly, and so maybe that was why I hadn't exploded. [Pause]

THERAPIST: And?

ALICIA: Well, I guess he believed me. Anyway, that talk ended well, too, and we made love for two nights running—which I know hasn't happened in I don't know how long. So that kind of cemented things. It's just been great since. I was worried that it wouldn't last, but so far it has. I'm still not feeling completely sure of things, but I'm a whole lot more sure.

From that point on, Alicia seemed clearly to have remitted from PTSD. The improvement in her marriage persisted, and perhaps strengthened, over the remaining sessions. Alicia now spontaneously acknowledged the importance of paying attention to her emotions, and made a point of telling people how she felt. As she became more adept at identifying and expressing frustrations, the anger no longer built up and she seemed to decompress. There were no further anger outbursts of consequence.

ALICIA: It's different now. You know, I always said to Dave and Joanie and Clara and my family that I loved them, but it was sort of canned. Now it feels real—warmer, closer. And I can tell that they hear it that way, too.

THERAPIST: What tells you?

ALICIA: It's the warmth in their responses. It's like we really mean it now. And—I know your next question: it feels much better.

THERAPIST: That's great.

Termination proceeded smoothly. She reported a general thawing of relations: not only at home, but at work, and with friends and relatives, she had "loosened up" and was far more relaxed, spontaneous, and genuine in her interactions, which sometimes still scared her, but she mainly felt a newly discovered pleasure. Even her public speeches felt more relaxed and "real." Although the therapist had not re-raised the issue of her childhood abuse, Alicia spontaneously began to express greater ambivalence about her mother in the present. An illustration of her greater comfort with emotion came in the penultimate session, session 13, when she burst into tears and told the therapist that, although she did not want to—or feel she needed to—continue therapy, she would miss coming to see him, and could never thank him for all the help he'd provided. The therapist did not interrupt this outflow of emotion, but later in the session reminded her that it was she who had taken the risks and done the hard work.

THERAPIST: I appreciate the thanks, but you really deserve most of the credit for getting better. (And so *much* better!) It's you who risked facing your feelings and risked expressing them to the people around you. I may have done some coaching, but you did the hard work between sessions and got the job done.

At termination, Alicia's CAPS score had decreased from 55 to 15 (remitted). At nine months follow-up, she remained well.

This case fits the general IPT pattern of treating a role transition, but also illustrates some of the adaptations of IPT to treating PTSD. Alicia provides a forceful example of a patient who was initially quite detached and numb with PTSD. The early treatment sessions focused on identifying and naming emotions. A determined patient who in some respects had been quite high functioning despite her chronic PTSD, she effectively put her emotions on the line in taking the subjectively great risk of expressing them to others around her. Thankfully, they responded positively, reinforcing her sense of mastery. By the end of 14 weeks, she was dramatically better in her emotional awareness and interpersonal functioning, and, in consequence, her PTSD had remitted. Her relationship with Dave had shifted from a role dispute to a social support.

The treatment did not go back to explore Alicia's evidently awful abusive childhood. Indeed, just how awful her childhood had been was never fully clarified, because she and her therapist did not explore it. Yet it had clearly been abusive enough to qualify as child abuse, a trauma meeting PTSD criterion A, and as the persuasive source of her disorder. Alicia showed little desire to dig up the past, and it proved unnecessary to do so, at least in order to acutely relieve her of her PTSD symptoms.

IPT in this treatment did not exhume the past either for the purposes of exposure therapy—reliving the trauma—or for psychodynamic interpretation. When Alicia raised, in passing, that she did not want to get angry the way her mother had, the therapist asked whether that was the only option, and whether there were not choices between complete suppression of and exploding in anger. Role play, and subsequent real-world interactions, indicated that there were.

CASE EXAMPLE 2

Victor, a 37-year-old single Hispanic, Roman Catholic, gay, male clerical worker, presented with the chief complaint, "I don't know why I'm here. I just hate my life." He had been referred by the MaleSurvivor organization, which supports men who have suffered sexual trauma. Victor met diagnostic criteria for both chronic PTSD, with a CAPS score of 75 (severe PTSD), and for major depression, with a Hamilton Depression Scale (Ham-D) score of 23 (severe). He reported having been repeatedly physically abused in childhood, beginning with his priest during his years of service as an altar boy. The priest had sworn him to secrecy and threatened him with damnation; when he finally told his mother, she did not believe his "blasphemy" and beat him. He had worked as a male prostitute, during which time he was raped on more than one occasion.

He now worked in a low-profile clerical job where he seemed to endeavor to stay out of trouble. Unassertive, visibly agitated, radiating helplessness, he felt picked on by his co-workers and superiors. One co-worker, Mark, gave him a particularly hard time, harassing him with gay slurs. Victor had given up on dating, as he had found himself pressed for unwanted sexual favors and had trouble saying no. He was quite isolated. Victor felt that he could not trust others—"They just take advantage of you"—and said he had no one he could confide in. His father had died when he was four. He only rarely saw his mother, who lived in Florida, or his two older, heterosexual brothers. He said he had never come out to them because he knew they would just reject him. Thus he had little available social support.

There was a family history of alcohol abuse and depression, and Victor acknowledged heavy drinking to assuage his pain. "I drink myself to sleep." He denied seizures, and more than occasional blackouts; and he denied other drug use. He had made three or four suicidal gestures in past years, superficially cutting his wrist when he felt numb and despairing. He met four of the required five criteria for borderline personality disorder. He had been treated in his youth for sexually transmitted diseases but was HIV-negative; his medical history was otherwise non-contributory.

Victor was a thin, handsome, alert, dark-haired, olive-skinned male, appearing his stated age; well groomed, wearing a subdued wardrobe. He appeared fidgety and mildly agitated, with timid, slightly effeminate movements. He rarely made eye contact, looking off to corners of the office. His speech was soft and hesitant, although fluent. His sentences tended to trail off. His mood was anxious and depressed, with a detached, nonlabile affect. His thinking was grossly goal-directed but distractible. He denied psychotic symptoms. Although he felt life was painful and mostly not worth living, he denied suicidal plans or intent. His insight was limited: he came for treatment because he had been referred, but felt he was just a damaged, useless person and had little hope for the future. "Some Victor—I'm a loser." His sensorium was clear.

The therapist gave Victor the diagnosis of PTSD as a treatable illness, noting that he was also quite depressed and that these conditions overlapped. "It's treatable, and it's not your fault. No one asks for PTSD, but you've been battered throughout your life, starting with that priest, and it's taken a toll." The therapist gave Victor a handout about IPT for PTSD (see Appendix) and noted that the disorder seemed to be hurting him in many areas of his life, making it hard for him to defend himself in interpersonal situations—particularly with Mark.

Victor had been working steadily at his current job for seven years, scraping by, always feeling inferior, inadequate, and put upon by others. His stance was passive, unassertive, non-confrontational. He reported that he didn't like trouble, didn't want to "get in trouble" by standing up to others. When asked about getting angry, he simply said he didn't. While many co-workers seemed to ignore him, others actively took advantage of him, dumping their work on him when they realized he would not actively object. Still others, like Mark, were openly hurtful, even sadistic. Mark greeted him with insults ("Watch it, fag!"), and spoke with open disrespect about him to others. He left garbage as well as extra work for Victor on Victor's desk. Although Mark did not outrank Victor in the company hierarchy, Victor tended to do this added work anyway; getting caught up in the work was at least an escape from the office pressure. This had gone on for at least a year.

THERAPIST: How do you feel about the way Mark treats you?
VICTOR: I just try to ignore it.
THERAPIST: That must be hard to do. Surely you have some reaction?

VICTOR: He's just not a nice guy.

THERAPIST: Uh-huh.

VICTOR: . . . He's mean.

THERAPIST: You certainly have made it sound like he's mean to you. *Really* mean. But what do you feel when he's mean? You must have an emotional reaction.

VICTOR: I don't know. I don't feel much of anything. I'm used to it.

THERAPIST: When he greets you with a slur, you don't have any feeling?

VICTOR: I guess I don't like it. It's not nice.

THERAPIST: No, it isn't. I don't blame you for not liking it. How do you feel towards *him*?

VICTOR: I don't know. I just feel numb, empty.

THERAPIST: When you say you don't like it, what's the name for that feeling?

VICTOR: Upset?

With this level of emotional detachment, progress was gradual, but over the course of the first few sessions, Victor seemed increasingly aware of feeling *something*: a little hurt, a little angry at Mark. In the third session, the therapist framed the problem as a role dispute: Victor was entitled to decent treatment from Mark (and everyone else) and wasn't getting it.

THERAPIST: As we've determined, you are suffering from PTSD and depression, treatable conditions that aren't your fault. You have a good chance of getting better in the course of these 14 sessions; this is only our third. As I understand it, you're in a very painful relationship with Mark, and to some degree also with other people around you. These are one-sided relationships in which they're taking advantage of you, being mean to you, not treating you well. We call this kind of painful relationship a *role dispute*. If we can figure out a way for you to renegotiate the relationship so that it's fairer and goes better, not only will your situation at work be better—feel safer and more secure—but your PTSD and depression symptoms are likely to improve, too: you'll have made your life better, and you'll feel better, too. I think there's a good chance that you can accomplish this in the coming weeks. Does that make sense to you?

VICTOR: It makes some sense, but I doubt I can do it.

THERAPIST: That kind of pessimism is the depression talking. I think your odds are pretty good. Worth a try?

VICTOR: Yes. Can't hurt.

Recognizing Victor's history of repeated abuse and revictimization, the therapist made a point of encouraging Victor to bring up any discomfort he might have in the therapy sessions ("If there's anything I do that bothers you, please let me know; it isn't intentional")—the therapist wouldn't be insulted, would in fact welcome his raising his feelings in the session. Victor relaxed a little bit after this encouragement, but he never raised objections to the treatment.

The therapist pointed out that one key way to know that he was being mistreated was through his feelings, the feelings that were starting to break through the numbness Victor had chronically reported. Anger and hurt were reactions to mistreatment. As Victor began to raise such feelings, the therapist spent several sessions normalizing them: "They're not 'bad' feelings; they're appropriate responses to the bad behavior of other people!" But Victor had so long been so passive, had so little experience in confrontation, that although he acknowledged the feelings, he remained hesitant to act on them. The therapist raised the concept of *transgression* (see Chapter 6) in an attempt to mobilize him.

THERAPIST: There are some written or unwritten laws of society that everyone knows: what's fair is fair, and what is unfair is unfair. There are some behaviors that everyone would agree are bad—that if someone else does it to you, you're right to be angry, and at the very least entitled to an apology. The way Mark treats you—the insults, the disrespect—that's just not the way any human being should treat another. You're standing on solid ground if you object to that.
VICTOR: That's an idea. An apology.

They role-played how Victor might handle this.

VICTOR: [hesitantly] "Mark, you have to stop insulting me all the time. You have to stop dumping stuff on my desk. No one should treat another person that way. You owe me an apology."
THERAPIST: How did that feel?
VICTOR: I don't know. Artificial. Pretty wimpy.
THERAPIST: Did you say what you wanted to say?
VICTOR: Yeah, the ideas were okay, it's the way it came out.
THERAPIST: What sounded wrong?
VICTOR: It just didn't sound forceful—he'd steamroll right over me if I said something like that.
THERAPIST: How would he do that?

VICTOR: He'd say, "Fuck you—you can't talk to me like that, you pussy!"

THERAPIST: That's ugly. But if he did that, how could you respond?

VICTOR: Respond? . . . I guess I could say, "That's the kind of talk no one should use—you owe me an apology." But it still sounds flat.

THERAPIST: So the content is good, but you're unhappy with the delivery?

VICTOR: Yeah.

THERAPIST: Well, let's try it again. How would you like to say it?

VICTOR: Stronger. Like [louder]—"Don't talk to me like that, you bully!"

THERAPIST: How was that?

VICTOR: A little better.

THERAPIST: How do you think he'd respond?

VICTOR: Well, I guess he might punch me, but really—I think he'd be shocked that I said anything. . .. Or maybe, "How dare you! Never talk to me like that again, you big bully, or I'm reporting you. And you owe me an apology."

The therapist commented that "bully" was a perfect description of Mark. They continued to role play over the next two sessions. ("And stop dumping your work on me—do it yourself!") Victor came to session 8 looking much brighter, and reporting that he had confronted another co-worker, Jim, with success. Jim said he was sorry, that he hadn't meant to bother him. This emboldened him to take on Mark, and that, too, went surprisingly well. Mark hadn't exactly apologized, but he had looked down, abashed. After one later short-lived attempt at braggadocio, Mark had left him alone. He was no longer putting junk or work on Victor's desk. Victor felt relieved, better about himself. Over the next weeks he reported that he actually felt good rather than fearful going to work. It was beginning to feel like a somewhat safer place. He felt better able to defend himself. Some people were even acting a little nice toward him.

With a new appreciation for the benefits of recognizing and expressing anger, Victor raised a new issue in session 10. His troubles had started with his molestation by his priest. He had been reading in the paper about the Church scandals. Maybe he deserved an apology from the Church? The therapist listened and asked him how he felt.

VICTOR: I think he treated me horribly, took advantage of his holy office to molest me and silence me. I'm still hurt, embarrassed, and angry. I think he *does* owe me an apology.

THERAPIST: I think you should trust your feelings.

Victor went to his parish and asked how to proceed. He also asked at MaleSurvivor, an organization familiar with this issue, which provided support, encouragement, and information. He lodged a formal complaint, which felt good. He also raised the topic of having closer, more open relations with his family, and role-played talking to one of his brothers. He did not, however, pursue that further.

Work continued to go well. Mark made no more trouble, and indeed Victor's standing up to him seemed to have led to a comeuppance: other workers showed their disapproval of Mark. It felt a lot safer. A co-worker asked Victor if he'd like to have lunch. He was nervous, but agreed. It went a little awkwardly, but pretty well. Victor began to feel friendly toward a few of his co-workers and, as he emerged from his defensive stance, they responded positively to him.

As treatment approached termination, Victor and his therapist discussed Victor's social life. The therapist wondered aloud: If he had made a safe space for himself at work, if he could use anger to react to disagreements and renegotiate relationships, might it be safe for Victor to risk social relationships? The rules of social functioning are vaguer than the job descriptions at work, but Victor seemed to have grasped the principle. Victor agreed that this was a goal for the future. By the time therapy ended, at 14 sessions, he was increasingly comfortable with work acquaintances but had not yet risked a romantic relationship. His CAPS score had decreased to 24, and he did not meet formal criteria for PTSD; his Ham-D score had fallen to 8, consistent with remission. There was no hint of borderline personality disorder symptoms. He had not cut himself. He felt life was worth living and had some hope for the future.

Victor did not call in at six months, but at the end of the year, the therapist received a long letter from him. Victor reported that all was well: he was feeling good, safer, more sure of himself, if still a little anxious—but not numb, not depressed, nothing like before. He had asked for and received a promotion at work, where he was getting along with other people. Mark had been transferred to another department, to general relief. Victor had spoken to his mother and one brother about his life, including raising the story of the priest. This time they had said they believed him, which had been very gratifying. He had received no word, no satisfaction from the Church. He had dated a little, but felt he still needed to work on that, and asked for a referral for further psychotherapy.

Patients with early childhood and repeated traumatizations often present like this: beaten down, passive, emotionally disconnected. There is a huge potential for growth in interpersonal functioning under such circumstances if the therapist can engage the patient's interest in his or her emotional life and its interpersonal meaning. Victor, who had never previously been in therapy, was in many ways a model patient: motivated, despite his anxious hesitancy; determined, despite the chronicity of his symptoms and the impoverishment of his environment. Perhaps feeling the pressure of the 14-week time limit, he made the most of his brief treatment.

Although the pattern of trauma Victor had suffered was evident, the treatment did not focus on recounting or reliving it, or on facing reminders of the trauma. IPT focused squarely on interpersonal functioning. If in the end Victor tried to confront the priest who had molested him, it was on his own initiative—not something the therapist had raised—and followed naturally from his having first confronted Mark at work. Note, too, that the therapist could have framed this case as either a role dispute or role transition, where the transition would have involved recovery from years of abuse. The role dispute format seemed preferable, given the current conflict Victor was enduring at work.

Victor was a research study patient, and treatment had to end at 14 weeks. He had nearly remitted at this point (technically, a CAPS score of 20 constitutes PTSD remission; but he no longer met *DSM-IV* criteria for either PTSD or a mood disorder). Nonetheless, he was just finding a new equilibrium, just taking new positive steps in his life. Had this not been a research protocol, continuation or maintenance IPT might have been helpful. When Victor wrote a year later, the therapist made that referral.

10

IPT for PTSD—Termination Phase and Maintenance

TERMINATION

The therapist should announce termination by session 10 or 11 of 14, although with fragile patients, it is often helpful to raise the issue earlier. Because patients know from the start that treatment is time-limited, they generally tolerate the ending of IPT well. If they are better, they may well not want to continue treatment. If IPT has not helped them in 14 weeks, it may realistically be time to switch to another treatment that might help the patient more.

The tasks of termination include:

- Consolidating the patient's gains in therapy, thereby
- Increasing a sense of competence once therapy ends
- Emotionally acknowledging the end of treatment
- Deciding on next steps

Consolidating Gains. The therapist helps the patient leave treatment with a sense of competence and confidence by reviewing gains the patient has made during treatment and emphasizing the patient's deserved credit for such gains. The patient's central role in such achievements is usually clear in IPT, as much of what happens during therapy obviously takes place in the patient's life outside the office. The therapist may be a good coach, but the patient has done the hard work and deserves the credit for improvement.

It's helpful to ask, "Why are you feeling better?" This leads to a review of crucial steps the patient has taken on the road to treatment response or remission. For patients with IPT, this will generally include:

- Moving from numb detachment and dissociation to risking emotional awareness
- An increasing sense of the normalcy, validity, and meaningfulness of feelings, particularly negative emotions such as anger, sadness, and anxiety
- Risking confrontation in expressing these feelings (generally after considerable role play)
- New interpersonal skills (self-assertion, expressing anger, asking for an apology)
- Key moments: such as Martina confronting Jamie; Leonard crying, and then talking to Rose; Alicia talking to Dave; Victor confronting Mark
- A (perhaps still shaky) sense of a stronger identity—as resilient, a survivor, with greater mastery of the environment—as the patient takes control of his or her life and symptoms recede

Reviewing these points helps reinforce interpersonal changes and skills that the patient will probably find adaptive in future. All of these maneuvers are likely to instill the patient with a greater sense of competence and of independence: having incorporated the IPT approach, the patient may no longer need treatment in order to function well and stay well. The therapist's goal is to ensure that the patient takes appropriate credit for his or her achievement.

It's also important to remind the patient that he or she has succeeded in treatment, taking charge of his or her life at a moment of great distress and perceived self-weakness. Recall that success experiences are a "common factor" important to treatment outcome (see Chapter 5).

Emotionally Acknowledging the End of Treatment. In announcing termination, the therapist generally says something like: "You may have feelings about our treatment ending, which I encourage you to bring up." Patients will do so to varying degrees. Termination is acknowledged as a bittersweet moment—"It's sad to break up a good team"—but also a graduation from acute treatment. That is, sadness is a social signal, reflecting the coming separation and loss of the therapeutic relationship. The sadness of termination may be usefully contrasted with grief associated with the trauma that precipitated PTSD, or (when appropriate) with depression.

It is fine to tell a patient that you've enjoyed working with him or her, as long as such self-disclosure is not used to cut off the patient's feelings about terminating. It's best to elicit those first.

Next Steps. Even much improved patients sometimes feel shaky in leaving treatment. Therapist and patient discuss risks of symptom recurrence and forecast ways of coping with future challenges. The patient should optimally leave treatment with a new recognition of the impact of the trauma he or she has suffered, its interpersonal sequelae, and with gains in and tools for further improving interpersonal functioning.

Termination is a time to anticipate future problems the patient may face and to discuss interpersonal coping strategies to deal with them. "What problems can you anticipate arising in future?"

For patients whose PTSD has really improved, the prognosis may actually be better than it is for major depression (Judd et al., 1998), which tends to recur in the absence of maintenance treatment (Frank et al., 1990). Patients whose PTSD gets better generally stay better unless they suffer a new trauma. A patient who understands how to handle interpersonal stressors by calling on social supports to express their feelings and gain validation may well be less likely to suffer a recurrence. Some patients may benefit from a shift in treatment from the current focus to treating comorbid disorders, or referral to another therapist for that purpose.

Patients who do not improve in acute (14-week) IPT for PTD, or who show minimal improvement but have considerable residual symptoms and need ongoing further treatment, should be referred appropriately. For IPT non-responders, this might include pharmacotherapy with serotonin re-uptake inhibitors (SRIs) and psychotherapies such as Prolonged Exposure, Cognitive Processing Therapy, or another empirically validated treatment. In our randomized treatment study, we offered non-responders to 14 weeks of study treatment a choice of one of the other study therapies (IPT, Prolonged Exposure, or Relaxation Therapy), medication, or a combination thereof. Many of those patients subsequently responded to this second course of treatment.

When patients with PTSD (or any diagnosis) do not improve, it is impor-tant to help them see that this lack of improvement is not a personal failure, but that the *treatment* has failed: no approach works for everyone, and there are alternative, effective treatments available. The approach is comparable to a failed pharmacotherapy trial: blame the treatment, not the patient, and find a different treatment that might work better. Under such circumstances, it is important to help patients recognize any gains they have made, and to help them fight off demoralization that might keep them from proceeding toward treatments that might help.

One way to do this in IPT is to review interpersonal progress, which may well have been significant: How has the patient learned to handle relation-ships differently? What skills has the patient applied in dealing with people with whom he or she had previously been detached and distant? The patient who has progressed in this area has fulfilled his or her part of the bargain in IPT: this is what we have been asking the patient to do. Symptoms are supposed to have improved as a result: if they have not, then (1) the patient still has gained some interpersonal skills, which is good; and (2) it should be clear that it is the therapy itself that has failed to deliver its promise, not the patient.

It is reasonable to ask a patient who is terminating treatment to check in with you in future. This simply adopts the general practitioner's approach to treatment: "Now that you're better, you can go home; if you feel ill again, please come back." This stance follows from the IPT emphasis that illness is treatable and not the patient's fault. You can also ask whether, if it's not an imposition, the patient could check in with you in 6 or 9 or 12 months to let you know how things are going. Most patients are happy to do so. This provides a sense of continuity even after treatment has formally ended, and indicates the therapist's ongoing interest in the patient's well-being.

MAINTENANCE TREATMENT

Several studies at the University of Pittsburgh have demonstrated that maintenance IPT, conducted as infrequently as once a month, can protect patients from recurrence of even highly recurrent major depressive disorder (e.g., Frank et al., 1990; Frank et al., 2007; Reynolds et al., 1999). Some patients may benefit significantly from acute IPT for major depression, yet remain at high risk of recurrence, either because of a history of multiple prior episodes or because of high residual depressive symptoms. For example, they may have improved in treatment from an initial Hamilton Depression Rating Scale score of 29 to a post-treatment score of 14, but at 14 remain on the cusp of major depression. For such patients, who already know the approach and their therapists, maintenance treatment makes clear clinical sense, and research has validated this. For such patients, the IPT approach is to terminate acute treatment and then re-contract for continuation or maintenance IPT: for example, once-monthly sessions for three years, or twice monthly sessions for two years.

How about ongoing treatment for PTSD? Many patients with PTSD improved in our IPT study, and yet many did not fully recover and might have benefitted from maintenance IPT therapy. Indeed, most patients with chronic PTSD who receive any empirically validated treatment do not remit and might benefit from further treatment. Our research trials simply tried to determine whether IPT worked acutely, a necessary first step before considering longer term treatment. Now that we have an initial positive answer supporting IPT, it would be helpful to know whether maintenance IPT works—but absent data, we simply cannot say. Because the National Institute of Mental Health is not funding expensive maintenance treatment trials these days, we will probably have no answer in the near future.

In clinical practice, it makes intuitive sense for a patient with PTSD who has improved in IPT but remains symptomatic to continue treatment with a therapist whom he or she has come to trust. To do so, the therapist should first conclude acute treatment as originally contracted, then set up a new schedule incorporating the patient's preference. How frequently would the patient like to meet? For how long an interval into the future? And with what goals? Maintenance IPT has the flexibility of switching problem areas to meet new interpersonal issues that may arise over the course of time. This maintenance approach has worked well for PTSD patients in my private practice who benefitted from acute IPT.

11

Difficult Situations and Special Circumstances

"The man who in a fit of melancholy kills himself today would have wished he lived had he waited a week."

—VOLTAIRE, *Philosophical Dictionary*

Like many individuals with other psychiatric diagnoses, patients with PTSD present potential clinical risks. The therapist needs always to keep these in mind in order to minimize them. Our treatment study minimized risk to some degree through study exclusion criteria (excluding substance dependence, for example), frequent evaluation of symptoms, and encouraging patients to tell us of crises.

DANGEROUSNESS

Suicide. Patients with PTSD, especially those with comorbid depression, carry the risk of clinical worsening and, as a worst outcome, suicide. Many have at least passive suicidal ideation, the feeling that life is too painful and not, or barely, worth living. None of the 14 patients in our open pilot trial (Bleiberg and Markowitz, 2005) and one of the 40 IPT patients in our randomized trial (Markowitz et al., 2015) attempted suicide. Suicidal ideation needs careful exploration, beginning with intake into treatment, to determine level of risk: Has the patient made previous attempts? Has he or she developed a plan for self-harm? Written a will? In our research, we asked therapists and evaluators to stay alert to suicide risk, assessed it on rating scales, asked treatment staff to report any meaningful suicide risk immediately, and subsequently discussed cases in supervision. The rare patients who reported worsening of suicidal ideation received additional assessments to ensure their safety.

Patients tend to feel suicidal because their level of distress feels unbearable and because they can foresee no future relief of this pain. The IPT approach to suicide includes:

- Recognizing suicidality as a treatable symptom of PTSD (and depression) that it's crucial for the patient to survive; once the patient feels better, suicidality is likely to fade
- Providing therapist availability
- Monitoring rather than avoiding the issue
- Maximizing safety

A therapist might say: "I know you're in a lot of pain, and that you don't see any way out. But you have an excellent chance of getting better, of beating PTSD, even if it's hard for you to see it right now. And *when you're feeling better, you'll want to live. It's important for you to stay alive long enough to get better.*" The therapist should explore contingency plans: what to do if the patient feels more out of control and seems likely to harm him- or herself. This might include social supports the patient can contact to talk about these painful feelings, and the therapist should make him- or herself available if the patient needs additional time and contact. It's important to remind patients that it's far preferable to go to an emergency room if necessary than to attempt suicide.

If the patient has a suicidal plan, it is important to try to remove access to self-destructive means: throwing out a cache of pills, with family supervision; removing firearms from a house, etc.

Once suicide risk has been assessed, it should be labeled a psychiatric symptom that is likely to improve as the patient's syndrome remits. The medical model of IPT is a useful explanation here, and the therapist's warm support and caring stance (again: "You need to stay in one piece long enough to get better; then you won't want to hurt yourself") should be protective to most patients. New onset or worsening of suicidal ideation should be examined in an interpersonal context: has something happened recently that has provoked greater dysphoria and suicidal symptoms?

In a research study, suicide risk triggers more frequent monitoring of symptoms. A patient with worsening suicidal risk might be withdrawn from the formal treatment protocol in order to receive additional treatment. Study therapy could then continue (the therapist shouldn't abandon the patient in a crisis) but be augmented by psychotropic medication, couples therapy, or whatever other interventions might be appropriate. In clinical practice, the goal is not to test the efficacy of IPT but to ensure that the patient gets better, rather than dying. Hence, therapists should not fear adding interventions, a "full court press" of psychiatric treatment, if necessary.

The only caveat is that a therapist should recognize suicidality as part of the range of psychopathology and need not abandon monotherapy with IPT simply because the patient reports it. A therapist who flinches prematurely, appearing panicked by patient symptoms, is not likely to imbue confidence in the patient. Thus therapeutic poise (Greenacre, 1957) and clinical judgment are important in deciding if and when to alter the treatment regimen. Mixing therapeutic elements into an eclectic slurry may actually confuse and discourage patients by blurring the thematic approach (Markowitz and Milrod, 2015; see Chapter 12).

In clinical practice, IPT is supportive, encouraging, and efficacious. These factors probably play an important role in averting suicide attempts and completion in at-risk patients. Blaming the disorder (PTSD or major depression) rather than the patient, recognizing the patient's suffering while emanating a concerned but calm, clinically optimistic but realistic, outlook (there is hope!), and providing encouragement and support are powerful therapeutic tools.

Violence. The modal diagnostic target of IPT over the decades has been major depressive disorder, a diagnosis strongly associated with suicide but much less so with harm to others. One aspect of PTSD is that some patients may lose control of bottled-up, violent impulses and may pose risks to others (e.g., McFall et al., 1999; Fehon et al., 2005).

The therapeutic approach to forestalling harm to others follows that of harm to self. Risk of violence needs frequent monitoring as a worst outcome, just as suicidal risk does. The therapist should rule out or, if present, try to mitigate contributing factors such as alcohol and drug use, which can be disinhibiting (Wilkinson et al., 2015), and traumatic brain injury (Stein et al., 2015) or other medical factors that might magnify impulsivity. As with suicide, therapist and patient should work to fight any opportunity to give in to the symptoms: for example, impeding access to weapons.

Most PTSD patients are frightened by their own potential for violence and may respond well to therapist support ("Please call me if you're worried you're going to feel out of control"). As with suicidal risk, the therapist's very gesture of offering availability often provides some reassurance to calm the patient, with the consequence of no calls and no dangerous outcomes. Therapist and patient should consider contingencies such as going to the emergency room if necessary ("What can you plan to do if you again start feeling like hurting her?").

Some patients can appear menacing and indeed may pose some level of risk – which is why they desperately need treatment. Your clinical judgment is crucial in such situations in gauging how to proceed. A veteran who reports having weapons at home, or who may be carrying a knife for self-protection to your office, may not only feel very anxious him- or herself, but may understandably cause you anxiety as well. The issue is best addressed directly. If the patient appears menacing, or if you feel menaced, you need to gauge the likelihood of this being a true threat. You do not want to overreact to (and thereby magnify) the patient's fears and risk, but you cannot ignore them. It is hard to conduct optimal therapy if you are worrying about your own safety.

Explore and identify the patient's affect: "How are you feeling coming in here?" . . . "If you're feeling fearful or unsafe, what options do we have to make these sessions more comfortable?" Acknowledging the emotion and treating it in measured, poised fashion is likely to calm both the patient and yourself. When a menacing patient enters your office, you may want to discuss the seating arrangement: would the patient rather be nearest to the door, or in a position to keep an eye on the door? Would the patient perhaps prefer that you leave the door ajar? (You will not want to sit between the patient and the door.)

I have had sessions with patients who were carrying knives; I did not feel particularly comfortable under these circumstances, but I did feel reasonably confident that the patient only had the weapon there for expected self-defense and was not likely to use it. We discussed the issue—enhancing the therapeutic relationship—and patients generally returned the next time without the knife. As a therapist, you will need to assess your own level of comfort: you cannot conduct effective psychotherapy if you feel too afraid for your own safety.

In certain high-risk situations, such as the patient's reporting an imminent, and subjectively out of control, plan to harm another person, a "duty to warn" or duty to protect takes effect (Johnson et al., 2014). This is one of the very rare circumstances where our legal duties supersede confidentiality; if the therapist cannot induce the patient to warn the potential victim, the therapist may do so him- or herself. This potential breach of confidentiality is a HIPAA issue that therapists should raise with patients at the start of any treatment; thankfully, its use is usually avoidable. Again, clinical judgement should prevail. Although our research studies excluded patients with the greatest risk of violence, there were no instances of violent behavior by study patients with chronic PTSD. They were far more likely to be victims of violence themselves.

Concern about violence should not obscure the IPT focus on validation and appropriate expression of feelings. Thus patients may have good reason to *feel* like punching or killing someone, and this is no crime as long as they do not act on the feeling. The underlying anger can be addressed, normalized, and hopefully channeled into a more socially appropriate outlet, which may well decrease violence risk.

COMORBIDITY

PTSD often presents amidst comorbid disorders. The most common psychiatric diagnostic consequences of trauma are PTSD, depression, and substance abuse, and patients may have any combination of these, in addition to other anxiety disorders, personality disorders, and other psychiatric and physical conditions. In general, pure PTSD without comorbidity is easier to treat than PTSD with comorbidity.

The first step in addressing comorbidity is to identify it through a comprehensive diagnostic evaluation before IPT formally begins. Because our research studies excluded patients with some forms of psychiatric and medical comorbidity, we have no data on how those conditions might affect the course of IPT for PTSD.

IPT was first tested as a treatment for major depressive disorder, and comorbid major depression is certainly no contraindication to treating patients with both disorders. Our research showed advantages for IPT relative to Prolonged Exposure therapy among patients with comorbid major depression, who were likelier to drop out of the latter treatment. On the other hand, patients with comorbid major depression overall fared less well across treatment conditions than did the half of patients who did not meet major depression criteria (Markowitz et al., 2015).

In contrast, IPT has not generally been effective as a treatment for serious substance use (e.g., Carroll, Rounsaville, & Gawin, 1991; Brache, 2012), although it may work in tandem with substance use treatment (Johnson and Zlotnick, 2012). Patients may report substance use momentarily relieves symptoms, or provides another attribution for their dysphoria; but in general it worsens their clinical state, increasing anxiety and depression over time as well as (often) the risk of impulsive, destructive behavior. Some patients with mild to moderate substance use disorders may respond to the therapist's encouragement to discontinue or minimize substance use so that the patient can benefit optimally from psychotherapy. Others may need referral to separate substance treatment programs.

Clinicians may expect to see paranoid ideation in many patients with chronic PTSD. Mistrust of people and environments is indeed part of the fabric of PTSD. In our study, patients with paranoid personality disorder at baseline frequently lost that diagnosis after 14 weeks of study treatment; hence that diagnosis should be made with caution (Markowitz et al., 2015b; see Chapters 1 and 7). On the other hand, patients with paranoid delusions accompanying PTSD will need antipsychotic medication; IPT alone is not equipped to handle psychosis, although its medical model makes IPT compatible with pharmacotherapy. If you plan to treat a psychotic patient with IPT, recognize that you have left the bounds of IPT research. I have done so on occasion with patients in my clinical practice, and my sense is that they have generally found IPT understandable and helpful. We have proceeded, however, far more gradually than in typical IPT, and generally have not used a time-limited framework. Patients with schizophrenia may frequently suffer trauma and develop PTSD, and we excluded many such patients from our research protocol (Amsel et al., 2012). Similarly, comorbid bipolar disorder would require pharmacotherapy (Frank et al., 2005).

A key aspect of comorbidity is its potentially dispiriting effect on the therapist. How much more comfortable to confront "pure" PTSD than a patient with a string of diagnoses! Yet our findings suggest that the length of the DSM diagnostic list should not discourage the therapist. More symptoms potentially mean more room for improvement. As our study results showed, many patients treated for PTSD responded with improvement in other diagnostic domains as well (Markowitz et al., 2015b).

REVICTIMIZATION

Individuals with PTSD have by definition suffered a trauma, and frequently this trauma is interpersonal. Some patients may have had interpersonal difficulties with self-assertion, expressing anger, or facing confrontations even before such events. In any event, PTSD symptoms compromise interpersonal interactions, making it hard for the patient to protect him- or herself. This raises the risk of revictimization, which only compounds maladaptive relationship problems. Patients may present with interpersonal circumstances ranging from current physical, sexual, or emotional abuse in relationships, to somewhat subtler but still destructive ongoing mistreatment in which the patient feels helplessly caught in a cycle of retraumatization.

Whereas many behavioral exposure therapies have excluded patients from treatment studies who are currently in abusive relationships, from an IPT perspective, it seems crucial to help patients trapped in such situations to recognize them and to either fight back, renegotiating a role dispute; or to escape, precipitating a role transition. It is crucial not to "blame the victim": individuals with PTSD really do feel helpless in these imprisoning interpersonal situations, for which IPT may provide a key to safety and better functioning. It is important not to see patients as masochists or losers, even if they characterize themselves with such terms.

In taking a history and interpersonal inventory, the IPT therapist should listen for and ask about such maladaptive, revictimizing patterns of interaction. Moreover, the potential for revictimization may well arise in the patient's life circumstances during the period of IPT treatment. Such a revictimization situation offers the patient and therapist a chance to anticipate difficulties, explore alternatives to the dysfunctional pattern, role-play them, and hopefully produce better outcomes that give the patient a greater sense of control over his or her life and symptomatic improvement.

OTHER PRACTICAL DIFFICULTIES

Patients who have been abused by previous therapists will have still more difficulty in trusting you than will other patients with PTSD. Asking about prior therapies is always an important aspect of taking a history, revealing important background about the patient's prior relationships with therapists and doctors and about the patient's expectations for the current treatment. If the patient has difficulty in trusting you as the therapist, you can acknowledge this as an interpersonal difficulty linked to PTSD (as opposed to making a transferential interpretation) and suggest that the problem is likely to lessen as treatment progresses. You can also encourage the patient to bring up discomfort with the therapeutic situation—the kind of expression of needs and wishes that IPT generally encourages:

> "If you feel uncomfortable during sessions, or if you feel I'm doing something anxiety-provoking or annoying, please tell me. I won't be offended. It's the kind of interpersonal issue that is often related to PTSD, and just the sort of thing we should be talking about."

Clearly, you must stand by this statement—not taking offense, and exploring any issues the patient might raise. It takes courage for a frightened and intimidated patient to confront a therapist, and the therapist should respect this, listen, and apologize if at fault.

If the patient describes sexual or other abuse by prior therapists, the therapist should (1) explore what happened (assuming the patient feels comfortable discussing this), (2) express dismay, (3) emphasize that this will not happen in the current therapy, and that the patient should feel free to bring up anything in the therapy that raises his or her mistrust or anxiety level. You can further ask the patient what ground rules might make proceeding in therapy less uncomfortable.

In this special case where therapy itself is (at least part of) the patient's trauma, some exposure to trauma memories may be unavoidable if therapy is to take place. Yet even here, the goal should be to address present functioning, rather than to review the past in ongoing fashion and detail or to systematically expose the patient to trauma reminders.

TELEPHONE CONTACTS

On one hand, IPT therapists want patients to feel that they are available, a reliable resource should emergencies or difficulties arise. Patients feel reassured when therapists respond quickly to their messages. Simply providing such availability often diminishes the actual number of calls received. On the other hand, it is best not to turn such calls into full sessions, and hence to limit their length.

If patients call in distress:

1. Try to return the call as soon as possible. (Apologize for any delays.) Listen empathically, but try to limit the call to a few minutes. Validate the patient's feelings as you would in a treatment session, and try to calm the patient.
2. Ascertain the patient's safety: Is the patient suicidal, homicidal, or considering an impulsive action? Encourage the patient to come in for an assessment or go to an emergency room if necessary. If you send the patient to the hospital, make it clear that you are not abandoning the patient—you will be in touch with the doctors there, and see the patient afterward—but simply trying to protect him or her.
3. Emphasize that the reason for the call—a recent life event or upsetting emotion, in all likelihood—is exactly the kind of thing worth discussing in your next session. Reconfirm the session time, or move the session to a more immediate, earlier time if that seems clinically warranted.
4. End by thanking the patient for calling: "I'm sorry you're having such a hard time. I'd rather know what's going on with you than not know."

We provided the above instructions about telephone calls to our research study therapists. They received very, very few calls over the course of a five-year study, suggesting that the offer of therapist availability comforts many very severely ill patients with chronic PTSD, and that making this offer may not lead to many actual calls.

12

Practical Issues

This chapter is modified from the research study manual, omitting sections about independent evaluators and various research protocol procedures. Many of the issues, however, apply to IPT for PTSD in clinical practice.

PRESCRIPTIONS: THINGS TO DO

The goal of the treatment is to provide 14 sessions of IPT-PTSD in as many weeks. Unavoidable delays due to vacation or patient scheduling may on occasion stretch out the treatment for an additional week or two, but the goal is to provide treatment within the 14-week envelope. Once-weekly sessions help maintain thematic continuity and therapeutic momentum.

1. *Schedule sessions:* Work out regular appointment times with your patient. The more you can provide a sense of safety and regularity, the better. If you know in advance that you (or the patient) will have interruptions in the treatment, it's preferable to spell them out ahead of time.
2. *Audiotape:* In our research, we audiotaped each session for supervisory and adherence purposes. (In clinical practice, you are probably less likely to do this, but I leave the point in this manual to indicate that it can be done. Therapists sometimes fear patients would object to such a procedure, but we found that even highly mistrustful individuals with PTSD were willing to be taped once they understood the purpose of the taping, the confidentiality protections, etc. A recording of a session is a far more accurate record than process notes and may be essential if you would like IPT supervision. Videotaping is even more informative and beneficial to adherence to technique than

audiotaping. If you plan to tape sessions, however, you should discuss this first, and have the patient sign an informed consent.) Place the digital tape recorder close to the patient and yourself, and turn off loud air conditioners and other background noise to ensure audibility of the tape. Turn the tape on *before* the patient enters the room, and do not turn it off until the patient has left.

Tapes will be reviewed in supervision and by independent evaluators to assure therapist adherence to treatment modality. You may reassure your patients that the recordings focus on *you*, the therapist, rather than on the patient, and that they will be erased once these technical reviews have been taken.

3. *Give the patient an IPT handout.* Some patients may find the IPT handout (see Appendix) a useful orientation for the treatment they are about to start.
4. *Write a progress note:* After each session, write a brief clinical progress note. We discouraged study therapists from taking notes during sessions, as everything was being recorded anyway on audiotape, and notes distract patient and therapist from eye contact and what should be a direct interpersonal encounter in the session.
5. *Ratings:* Tell the patient at the start of treatment that you will periodically ask questions (and/or provide self-report questionnaires) to see how treatment is progressing. You and your patient both may benefit from knowing how the patient is progressing. Patients should be rated at regular intervals using assessments for PTSD and, if appropriate, comorbid diagnoses such as major depressive disorder (as they were in our study by independent evaluators at New York State Psychiatric Institute). For PTSD, you might administer the CAPS-5 (Weathers et al., 2013a) or the self-report PCL-5 (Weathers et al., 2013) at the initial evaluation, at mid-treatment (week 7), at the end of acute treatment (week 14), and subsequently if treatment continues. For depression, the Hamilton Depression Rating Scale (Hamilton, 1960) or Beck Depression Inventory–II (BDI-II; Beck et al., 1996) can be used.

PROSCRIPTIONS: THINGS NOT TO DO

Our research study was very concerned with keeping the therapists who were conducting IPT, Prolonged Exposure, and Relaxation Therapy pure in their delivery, the three therapies distinct from one another. Hence, we cautioned IPT therapists to adhere to IPT and to avoid the techniques of the competing therapies. If you are a therapist using this manual in a research study comparing IPT to other treatments, this will remain true. Therapy should be recorded and evaluated to measure therapist adherence. Without such monitoring, there is no way to demonstrate that IPT therapists are doing IPT, and other therapists other therapies.

Even if you are not a research therapist, however, and are instead treating patients in clinical practice, the recommendations remain basically the same. Eclectic therapy tends to be weaker therapy: it loses its programmatic crispness, its thematic coherence (Markowitz & Milrod, 2015). Mixing IPT with other treatment elements may feel like you're doing more, but sometimes less is more. Particularly in a brief psychotherapy, it's important to convey organized principles to patients that they can understand and continue to use when they leave. If, six months after finishing treatment, your patient faces a difficult life situation, she or he is likely to fare better having a clear picture (interpersonal, cognitive, psychodynamic, or otherwise) of how to respond. Thus blending therapies may unintentionally breed confusion.

1. *Do not encourage exposure to traumatic reminders.* As already noted, exposure is not the focus or mechanism of IPT. Part of our interest is to show that IPT can treat PTSD without requiring the exposure exercises common to other validated PTSD therapies. If the patient decides to confront reminders of trauma on his or her own, that's fine, but you should not prompt the patient to do so. The focus of IPT is on interpersonal interactions in the present.
2. *Do not assign homework.* The other therapies will be doing this. The only homework of IPT is to resolve the interpersonal focus (e.g., role transition) in the course of the 14 weeks of treatment. Not providing specific homework assignments week to week has an advantage. If you assign no specific homework, the patient cannot fail to complete it, an outcome that would worsen the prognosis of behavioral therapies.
3. You should obviously not encourage the patient to do progressive muscle relaxation or breathing exercises, as the relaxation therapists will.
4. Do not engage in psychodynamic interventions such as dream or transference interpretation. Again, if the patient offers you a dream during a session, you can help the patient explore its manifest interpersonal content—but focus on the interpersonal interactions and emotions and then bring the treatment around to current waking events.

5. When you have succeeded in eliciting a strong negative affect from a patient, do not rush to do anything. Sit with it, let the patient sit with it, and give the patient the therapeutic opportunity to *reflect*: to tolerate and understand the emotion.

When in doubt, discuss what you can and can't do with your supervisor.

13

Training in IPT for PTSD

How much training does one need in order to conduct IPT adherently and competently? What constitutes "certification" in IPT? These two questions have been points of controversy over the forty year history of this treatment (Weissman et al., 2007; Markowitz & Weissman, 2012). Some early training research indicated that already experienced psychotherapists could adapt well to using IPT to treat patients following a single supervised pilot case (Rounsaville et al., 1986, 1988). In my experience, this has been true for some therapists. Other therapists benefit from at least a second supervised, successfully conducted case, which may also provide experience in working in a different problem area (e.g., grief vs. role dispute) or with a different target diagnosis.

Adherence to IPT can be determined by assessment of taped sessions (Hollon et al., 1984; Markowitz et al., 2000). Researchers have historically determined competence based on adherence and clinical supervision. Standards for training currently vary by country. Some countries have their own IPT societies and have set up requirements for training. The most developed training guidelines come from the United Kingdom (http://www.iptuk.net/). In the United States, where therapists receive certification by professional degree (M.D., Ph.D., L.C.S.W., R.N.) rather than by psychotherapy, there is no such thing as formal certification in IPT; and this holds true in much of the rest of the world. The International Society for Interpersonal Psychotherapy (listserv: isipt-list@googlegroups.com) provides information about IPT around the world, including posting announcements of training courses, but it specifically eschews any claim to certifying therapists in IPT.

My recommendations for training in IPT for PTSD are as follows:

1. *General clinical experience.* If you want to treat PTSD, it helps to have had some experience in working with patients who have the disorder. You will do a better job treating patients in IPT if you feel familiar with the target disorder. It's hard to learn two domains at once. An

important common factor of therapy (Frank, 1971) is *therapeutic poise*: the ability to remain composed when a patient reveals something painful or alarming (Greenacre, 1957; Markowitz & Milrod, 2011) or acts in an upsetting way in a session. If you stay reasonable and calm and react appropriately, the patient is likely to feel reassured. You will be more likely to maintain that pose if you have familiarity with PTSD.

Most therapists do not learn IPT as a first therapy, but come to it having first received training in psychodynamic psychotherapy or Cognitive Behavioral Therapy.

2. *General competence in IPT.* Perhaps it's my prejudice based on the way I learned IPT, but I feel it makes sense to start at the beginning: to first use IPT where it was first used, and remains most used—as a treatment for major depressive disorder. Thus I recommend that therapists first treat a depression case, then branch out. Leaving aside the thorny question of certification, the general approach to training is threefold (Weissman et al., 2007):

   a. *Read a manual*: For general IPT, I recommend Weissman et al., 2000, or Weissman et al., 2007. If you have come this far in this book, you will have already read an IPT manual. The manual provides initial orientation to the treatment, then serves as a protocol and reference guide as you actually conduct treatments.

   b. *Attend a workshop*: IPT experts offer courses in various settings, ranging from freestanding workshops to professional organizational meetings such as the American Psychiatric Association Annual Meeting. The International Society for Interpersonal Psychotherapy holds biennial meetings with various training workshops. A one- or two-day course, in conjunction with having read a manual, often helps orient therapists and organize their thinking about the treatment. Such workshops often include videotapes of patient sessions or role plays among participants that can bring aspects of the treatment to life.

   c. *Supervision*: The only way to really learn a psychotherapy is to do it. The best way to practice it, at least at first, is with feedback, so that you know whether you are actually doing IPT or not. Supervised cases should include:

      i. Audio- or videotaping sessions, inasmuch as process notes are unreliable (Chevron & Rounsaville, 1983) and the supervisor can provide more accurate help if you and the supervisor have an accurate record of the session;

    ii. Using the manual as a guide;

   iii. Serial assessment of patients to measure symptomatic improvement;

   iv. Regular (ideally, weekly) supervision sessions based on review of the taped treatment sessions.

Two kinds of supervision have yielded good IPT therapists. The more expensive involves hiring an IPT expert for individual or group supervision. An alternative that has worked quite well for research groups in Canada, the Netherlands, and elsewhere has been group peer supervision. Interested therapists who have general psychotherapy experience meet regularly together and, using the above supervisory elements, supervise one another's taped cases based on reading an IPT manual.

3. *What about training in IPT specifically for PTSD?* This diagnosis is new for IPT, and essentially all the therapists trained in IPT for PTSD to date were trained to conduct research studies (e.g., Krupnick et al., 2008; Campanini et al., 2010; Markowitz et al., 2015). A purpose of this manual is to disseminate information about the adaptation of IPT for PTSD to a wider clinical population. IPT/PTSD workshops began in London in 2015 and 2016 and hopefully will continue.

14

Conclusion

Where Do We Go from Here?

This manual was first written before the open trial of IPT for PTSD we published in 2005 (Bleiberg & Markowitz, 2005), was fleshed out for the larger randomized controlled trial we published in 2015 (Markowitz et al., 2015), and is further expanded now. The principles of this adaptation have remained constant throughout, and remain congruent with earlier IPT manuals that focused primarily on major depression (Klerman et al., 1984; Weissman et al., 2000, 2007). Because research on IPT for PTSD is limited and still preliminary, readers should surely not hold this book infallible or complete.

There is so much we do not yet know. To really confirm the efficacy of acute (14-week) individual IPT for PTSD requires a confirmatory, randomized replication trial (Flay et al., 2005), ideally by a separate research group. We do not yet know whether IPT has similar efficacy in treating PTSD in military personnel as in civilians, although we hope to explore this in an upcoming study. We do not know the optimal dosage of IPT for PTSD: is 14 weeks ideal, too brief, or too long? We have no data on whether IPT augmentation with medication (or vice versa) would have greater benefit than either treatment alone (cf. Schneier et al., 2012). And, as noted in Chapter 10, we do not know whether maintenance IPT might benefit patients who respond to acute treatment, yet continue to have troublesome PTSD symptoms.

We also hope to glean more findings from the research we have already done. A rich database may yield findings about mediators or moderators of IPT, neuroimaging findings, follow-up data (did patients who improved stay better?), and other related outcomes.

We also have not yet demonstrated *why* or *how* IPT works, for PTSD or other disorders. Theories abound, but no proof of the mechanism exists (Lipsitz & Markowitz, 2013; Markowitz et al., 2015). We speculate that, in addition to its beneficial effects on social support and social functioning, IPT works through greater emotional understanding of one's interpersonal life and one's illness, which may be measurable through *symptom-specific reflective function* (Rudden et al., 2009), a measure of the patient's emotional understanding of his or her PTSD symptoms, which we would expect to change more in affect-focused IPT than in an exposure-based treatment (see Chapter 4). We hope to test this hypothesis in an upcoming research trial. Knowing more about the active processes of IPT might allow a refinement of the treatment approach.

To come full circle, let's give one last thought to exposure. IPT clearly does not work through structured exercises of graded exposure to trauma reminders. Think, though, about what happens when a patient does such an exposure task. The patient faces a feared cue, has a rush of emotion, and then, if the patient does not flee, habituates: that is, the patient recognizes that the trauma reminder is no longer dangerous, and the emotions subside. IPT for PTSD does not do this, but it may have a parallel effect. In working on affect attunement, the IPT therapist elicits a similar range of the patient's emotions in response to quotidian interpersonal encounters. A patient with PTSD may feel a crescendo of anxiety, anger, or some combination of negative effects during a not-truly-dangerous interchange with a co-worker, family member, or friend. Or just recounting this incident in the session may evoke such emotions. By letting the patient sit with and reflect on these feelings, the IPT therapist has different aims than the exposure therapist, such as helping the patient to understand the interpersonal meaning of such feelings. Yet toleration of affect is, in a sense, a form of exposure. Conversely, exposure therapy implicitly teaches patients not just that trauma cues are not dangerous, but that the feelings they evoke are not so dangerous either. Thus IPT and exposure therapy differ considerably in approach and technique, but they target the same disorder and inevitably overlap to a degree.

It further remains to be seen whether IPT for PTSD will disseminate into general practice as an alternative to exposure-based treatments. To some degree, that may depend upon readers of this book who try using IPT for PTSD in their practice.

Patient Handout for IPT-PTSD

INTERPERSONAL PSYCHOTHERAPY (IPT) FOR POSTTRAUMATIC STRESS DISORDER (PTSD)

A. **What is PTSD?** Posttraumatic stress disorder (PTSD), a distressing psychiatric illness, results from one or more extremely upsetting, traumatic events. The trauma might be, for example, an assault by another person, a natural disaster like a tornado, witnessing a death, or combat experience. PTSD is common, affecting 10% of American women and 5% of men. PTSD is a *medical illness* and *not your fault*—no one wants to have it. Even though its symptoms can make you feel shattered and hopeless, it's a *treatable disorder,* and you have a very good chance of getting better. Not only have you already suffered a terrible trauma, but having PTSD means that the traumatic event continues to haunt your life. If the world once felt secure and predictable, it no longer does. PTSD tends to make the world seem a dangerous and uncertain place. PTSD can make it hard to trust your environment or anyone in it. You may become preoccupied with re-experiencing the trauma in thoughts, flashbacks, or dreams. You may find yourself avoiding things that remind you of the trauma. You may feel detached, cut off from people and your feelings, with less interest in the present and the sense that there's not much of a future. You may feel constantly on alert, jumpy, and easily angered. PTSD can also interfere with sleep and ability to concentrate. "Adding insult to injury," PTSD symptoms keep bothering you long after the event has passed.

B. **Treating PTSD.** There are several ways to treat PTSD. The approach we are offering you is called *Interpersonal Psychotherapy (IPT)*, a 14-week talking therapy that has been well tested and has shown benefits in treating major depression and other psychiatric conditions.

IPT is a simple, powerful treatment that we think has a good chance of helping you recover from what you've been through. Initial treatment research suggests that it may work as well as other, exposure treatments without requiring you to face fearful memories of your past trauma.

C. **Basic Principles.** IPT is based on a few key ideas:

1. **PTSD is a medical illness.** It is not your fault, not something you brought upon yourself. It is not who you are, not a flaw in your character. And, although you may feel hopeless about getting better at times, PTSD is *treatable*. There is a good chance that you may feel much better as treatment proceeds. In our initial study, all patients showed some improvement, more than 80% got much better, and 44% had essentially no remaining symptoms (reached remission). So there is real hope.

2. **Feelings and symptoms are connected to life events.** Just as your PTSD symptoms began with a traumatic event, *how you feel is usually connected to what's going on in your life*. When bad things happen, people feel bad; when good things happen, they tend to feel better. The reverse principle is also true: *how you're feeling affects what happens in your life*. If your mood is anxious or down or numb, it's hard to focus on activities, participate in them, and enjoy them. You can miss out on what's going on, which of course only makes you feel worse. IPT focuses on this connection between what's happening in your life and how you're feeling. Your therapist will work with you to understand these connections between mood and events and help you come up with ways to deal with them.

3. **IPT focuses on the present, not the past.** Some therapies dig up painful events from earlier in your life. Although we know that you have had such painful events (such past traumas define PTSD), you and your IPT therapist will not focus on them. Instead, the focus will be on *how you are functioning now, how the symptoms of PTSD are making it hard to function, and how you can overcome those symptoms.*

D. **What will your therapist want to know?** At the beginning of treatment, your IPT therapist will want to know something about who you are and what you've been through.

- How are you feeling?
- What is your current situation?
- Who are the important people in your life? How have you been getting along with them?
- What happened to you that led to PTSD?

- Have there been other traumas in your life?
- How have relationships changed, and how has your life changed, since the PTSD began?
- How would you like things to change during treatment? What would make your life better?

E. **How IPT works.** Each week for 14 weeks, your therapist will meet with you for about 50 minutes. It's important to try to meet regularly to maintain momentum in the treatment. If there are unavoidable vacations or other breaks during the treatment, your therapist will work with you to try to reschedule sessions.

1. Your therapist will be interested in
   - *how you're feeling* (anxious? down? angry?), and
   - *how your feelings may be linked to things that have happened during the week* between sessions.

For example: encounters you've had with other people, pleasant and unpleasant events, and how they affected you emotionally. Again, the connection between feelings and your life situations is crucial. *Feelings are useful signals about your situation.* If someone does something upsetting, you may feel hurt or angry. There is no such thing as a "bad" feeling.

We understand that, because of PTSD, you may have trouble feeling your feelings. IPT is designed to help you get back in touch with them.

2. After a few sessions, you and your therapist will choose one key area in your life to focus on: either *grief,* a *role dispute,* or a *role transition.* Each of these categories describes life situations that might have contributed to your developing PTSD, or else may have resulted from PTSD.
   - *Grief* means that PTSD started when someone close to you died, and you have had trouble dealing with that terrible loss.
   - A *role dispute* is an interpersonal struggle you may be having with someone close to you.
   - A *role transition* is a major change in life, including having suffered a disturbing trauma, moving to a new place, starting or ending a relationship, starting or ending a job, or developing a serious illness.

3. You and your therapist can explore how your PTSD affects your daily life situations, the emotions that arise in those situations, and what you can do to handle them more comfortably and effectively. The time that you're in therapy is *a good time to take "safe risks"*: to try out new ways of handling situations with other people and then discuss the results in therapy.

4. Your therapist will also be interested in people around you who may be able to provide you with *social support*, which helps protect against PTSD symptoms and aids in recovery from PTSD.

5. If you should feel uncomfortable during a session, don't hesitate to tell your therapist what's bothering you, including anything the therapist is doing that you don't like. Your therapist will be sympathetic and won't be offended.

F. **What IPT doesn't do.** Some therapies for PTSD ask patients to remember and relive their traumas in detail. This can be effective treatment, but it's not easy. *IPT does not ask you to relive the painful trauma* or traumas you've been through over and over. Instead, your treatment will focus on how you can feel better and function in the present, not letting past trauma keep you from having a healthy present and future. We want you to help regain a realistic sense of trust in yourself and in your interactions with the people and situations you face in daily life.Your IPT therapist also won't assign you homework to do week to week. Your therapist will encourage you to explore different ways of handling situations, though. The goal of treatment is to help you regain health, to relieve you of symptoms, and to restore a sense of control over what's going on in your life.

G. **Ratings.** Your therapist will periodically ask you questions or give you a questionnaire to see how you are doing, and how the symptoms of PTSD are shifting. This is important in order to see how much the treatment is helping you.

Therapist _____   Contact Number _____

REFERENCES

Aakvaag HF, Thoresen S, Wentzel-Larsen T, Røysamb E, Dyb G: Shame and guilt in the aftermath of terror: the Utøya Island study. *J Trauma Stress*. 2014;27:618–621.

Amaya-Jackson L, Davidson JR, Highes DC, et al.: Functional impairment and utilization of services associated with posttraumatic stress in the community. *J Trauma Stress*. 1999;12:709–24.

American Psychiatric Association: *Diagnostic and Statistical Manual of Mental Disorders*, 3rd ed. Washington, DC: American Psychiatric Association, 1980.

American Psychiatric Association: *Diagnostic and Statistical Manual of Mental Disorders*, 4th ed. Washington, DC: American Psychiatric Association, 1994.

American Psychiatric Association: *Diagnostic and Statistical Manual of Mental Disorders*, 5th ed. Arlington, VA: American Psychiatric Association, 2013.

American Psychiatric Association: Practice guideline for the treatment of patients with acute stress disorder and posttraumatic stress disorder. *Am J Psychiatry*. 2004;161(suppl):11.

American Psychiatric Association: *The American Psychiatric Association Guidelines for the Psychiatric Evaluation of Adults*, 3rd ed. Arlington, VA: American Psychiatric Association, 2015.

Amsel L, Hunter N, Kim S, Fodor KE, Markowitz JC: Does a trauma focus encourage patients with psychotic symptoms to seek treatment? *Psychiatric Serv*. 2012;63:386–389.

Barnicot K, Wampold B, Priebe S: The effect of core clinician interpersonal behaviors on depression. *Affect Disord*. 2014;167:112–117.

Beck AT, Steer RA, Brown GK: *Manual for the Beck Depression Inventory–II*. San Antonio, TX: Psychological Corporation, 1996. To obtain: Harcourt Assessment, Inc., 19500 Bulverde Road, San Antonio, Texas 78259. Phone: 1-800-211-8378; Fax: 1-800-232-1223.

Beckham JC, Lytle BL, Feldman ME: Caregiver burden in partners of Vietnam war veterans with posttraumatic stress disorder. *J Consult Clin Psychol*. 1996;64:1068–1072.

Blake DD, Weathers FW, Nagy LM, et al.: The development of a clinician-administered PTSD scale. *J Trauma Stress*. 1995;8:75–90.

Bleiberg KL, Markowitz JC: Interpersonal psychotherapy for posttraumatic stress disorder. *Am J Psychiatry*. 2005;162:181–183.

Bowlby JL: *Attachment and Loss*. London: Hogarth, 1969.

Brache K: Advancing interpersonal therapy for substance use disorders. *Am J Drug Alcohol Abuse*. 2012;38:293–298.

Brady K, Pearlstein T, Asnis GM, et al.: Efficacy and safety of sertraline treatment of posttraumatic stress disorder: a randomized controlled trial. *JAMA*. 2000;283: 1837–1844.

Breslau N, Kessler RC, Chilcoat HD, Schulz LR, Davis GC, Andreski P: Trauma and posttraumatic stress disorder in the community: the 1996 Detroit Area Survey of Trauma. *Arch Gen Psychiatry*. 1998;55:626–632.

Brewin CR, Andrews B, Valentine JD: Meta-analysis of risk factors for posttraumatic stress disorder in trauma-exposed adults. *J Consult Clin Psychol*. 2000;68: 748–766.

Campanini RF, Schoedl AF, Pupo MC, Costa AC, Krupnick JL, Mello MF: Efficacy of interpersonal therapy-group format adapted to post-traumatic stress disorder: an open-label add-on trial. *Depress Anxiety*. 2010;27:72–77.

Carroll KM, Rounsaville BJ, Gawin FH: A comparative trial of psychotherapies for ambulatory cocaine abusers: relapse prevention and interpersonal psychotherapy. *Am J Drug Alcohol Abuse*. 1991;17:229–247.

Chevron ES, Rounsaville BJ: Evaluating the clinical skills of psychotherapists. A comparison of techniques. *Arch Gen Psychiatry*. 1983;40:1129–1132.

Cloitre M, Koenen KC, Cohen LR, Han H: Skills training in affective and interpersonal regulation followed by exposure: A phase based treatment for PTSD related to childhood abuse. *J Consult Clin Psychol*. 2002;70:1067–1074.

Cloitre M, Scarvalone P, Difede JA: Posttraumatic stress disorder, self- and interpersonal dysfunction among sexually retraumatized women. *J Trauma Stress*. 1997;10:437–452.

Cloitre M, Stovall-McClough KC, Miranda R, Chemtob CM: Therapeutic alliance, negative mood regulation, and treatment outcome in child abuse-related posttraumatic stress disorder. *J Consult Clin Psychol*. 2004;72:411–416.

Cloitre M, Stovall-McClough KC, Nooner K, et al.: Treatment for PTSD related to childhood abuse: a randomized controlled trial. *Am J Psychiatry*. 2010;167:915–924.

Davidson JRT, Hughes D, Blazer D, George LK: Posttraumatic stress disorder in the community: an epidemiological study. *Psychol Med*. 1991;21:1–19.

DiMascio A, Weissman MM, Prusoff BA, Neu C, Zwilling M, Klerman GL: Differential symptom reduction by drugs and psychotherapy in acute depression. *Arch Gen Psychiatry*. 1979;36:1450–1456.

Endicott J, Nee J, Harrison W, et al.: Quality of Life Enjoyment and Satisfaction Questionnaire: a new measure. *Psychopharmacol Bull*. 1993;29:321–326.

Falkenström F, Markowitz JC, Jonker H, et al.: Can psychotherapists function as their own controls? Meta-analysis of the crossed therapist design in comparative psychotherapy trials. *J Clin Psychiatry*. 2013;74:482–491.

Fehon DC, Grilo CM, Lipschitz DS: A comparison of adolescent inpatients with and without a history of violence perpetration: impulsivity, PTSD, and violence risk. *J Nerv Ment Dis*. 2005;193:405–411.

Flay BR, Biglan A, Boruch RF, et al.: Standards of evidence: criteria for efficacy, effectiveness and dissemination. *Prev Sci*. 2005;6:151–175.

Foa EB, Keane TM, Friedman MJ (Eds.): *Effective Treatments for PTSD*. New York: Guilford, 2000.

Foa EB, Kozak MJ: Emotional processing of fear: exposure to corrective information. *Psychol Bull*. 1986;99:20–35.

Foa EB, Rothbaum BO, Riggs DS, Murdock TB: Treatment of posttraumatic stress disorder in rape victims: a comparison between cognitive-behavioral procedures and counseling. *J Consult Clin Psychology*. 1991;59:715–723.

Foa EB, Rothbaum BO: *Treating the Trauma of Rape: Cognitive-Behavioral Therapy for PTSD*. New York: Guilford, 1998.

Fonagy P, Gergely G, Jurist E, Target M: *Affect Regulation, Mentalization and the Development of the Self*. New York: Other Press, 2002.

Frank E, Kupfer DJ, Buysse DJ, et al.: Randomized trial of weekly, twice-monthly, and monthly interpersonal psychotherapy as maintenance treatment for women with recurrent depression. *Am J Psychiatry*. 2007;164:761–767.

Frank E, Kupfer DJ, Perel JM, et al.: Three-year outcomes for maintenance therapies in recurrent depression. *Arch Gen Psychiatry*. 1990;47:1093–1099.

Frank E, Kupfer DJ, Thase ME, et al.: Two-year outcomes for interpersonal and social rhythm therapy in individuals with bipolar I disorder. *Arch Gen Psychiatry*. 2005;62:996–1004.

Frank J: Therapeutic factors in psychotherapy. *Am J Psychotherapy*. 1971;25:350–361.

Freud S: *The Interpretation of Dreams*, 3rd ed. Translated by AA Brill. New York: Macmillan, 1913.

Gibbon M, Spitzer RL, Williams JBW, et al.: *Structured Clinical Interview for DSM-IV Axis II Disorders (SCID-II)*. Washington, DC: American Psychiatric Publishing, 1997.

Greenacre P: The childhood of the artist—libidinal phase development and giftedness. *Psychoanal Stud Chil*. 1957;12:47–72.

Hamilton M: A rating scale for depression. *J Neurol Neurosurg Psychiatry*. 1960;25: 56–62.

Hembree EA, Foa EB, Dorfan NM, Street GP, Kowalski J, Tu X: Do patients drop out prematurely from exposure therapy for PTSD? *J Trauma Stress*. 2003;16:555–562.

Hoge CW, Riviere LA, Wilk JE, Herrell RK, Weathers FW: The prevalence of posttraumatic stress disorder (PTSD) in US combat soldiers: a head-to-head comparison of DSM-5 versus DSM-IV-TR symptom criteria with the PTSD checklist. *Lancet Psychiatry*. 2014;1:269–277.

Hollon SD: *Final Report: System for Rating Psychotherapy Audiotapes*. Bethesda, MD: US Department of Health and Human Services, 1984.

Holmes TH, Rahe RH: The Social Readjustment Rating Scale. *J Psychosom Res*. 1967; 11:213–218.

Horowitz LM, Rosenberg SE, Baer BA, Ureno G, Villasenor VS: Inventory of interpersonal problems: psychometric properties and clinical applications. *J Consult Clin Psychol*. 1988;56:885–892.

Institute of Medicine Committee on Treatment of PTSD: *Treatment of Posttraumatic Stress Disorder: An Assessment of the Evidence*. Washington, DC: National Academy of Sciences, 2008.

Jacobsen E: *Progressive Relaxation*. Chicago, IL: University of Chicago Press, 1938.

Janoff-Bulman R: *Shattered Assumptions: Toward a New Psychology of Trauma.* New York: Free Press, 1992.

Jayawickreme N, Cahill SP, Riggs DS, et al.: Primum non nocere (first do no harm): symptom worsening and improvement in female assault victims after prolonged exposure for PTSD. *Depress Anxiety.* 2014;31:412–419.

Johnson JE, Zlotnick C: Pilot study of treatment for major depression among women prisoners with substance use disorder. *J Psychiatr Res.* 2012;46:1174–1183.

Johnson R, Persad G, Sisti D: The Tarasoff rule: the implications of interstate variation and gaps in professional training. *J Am Acad Psychiatry Law.* 2014;42:469–477.

Judd LL, Akiskal HS, Maser JD, et al.: A prospective 12-year study of subsyndromal and syndromal depressive symptoms in unipolar major depressive disorders. *Arch Gen Psychiatry.* 1998;55:694–700.

Kardiner A, Spiegel H: *War Stress and Neurotic Illness.* New York: Hoeber, 1947.

Kehle-Forbes SM, Meis LA, Spoont MR, Polusny MA: Treatment initiation and dropout from prolonged exposure and cognitive processing therapy in a VA outpatient clinic. *Psychol Trauma.* 2016;8:107–114.

Kessler RC, Berglund P, Demler O, Jin R, Merikangas KR, Walters EE: Lifetime prevalence and age-of-onset distributions of DSM-IV disorders in the National Comorbidity Survey Replication. *Arch Gen Psychiatry.* 2005;62:593–602.

Kessler RC, Chiu WT, Demler O, Walters EE: Prevalence, severity, and comorbidity of 12-month DSM-IV disorders in the National Comorbidity Survey Replication. *Arch Gen Psychiatry.* 2005;62:617–627.

Kessler RC, Sonnega A, Bromet E, Hughes M, Nelson CB: Posttraumatic stress disorder in the National Comorbidity Survey. *Arch Gen Psychiatry.* 1995;52:1048–1060.

Klerman GL, Weissman MM, Rounsaville BJ, Chevron ES: *Interpersonal Psychotherapy for Depression.* New York: Basic Books, 1984.

Krupnick JL, Green BL, Stockton P, Miranda J, Krause E, Mete M: Group interpersonal psychotherapy for low-income women with posttraumatic stress disorder. *Psychother Res.* 2008;18:497–507.

Krupnick JL, Sotsky SM, Simmens S, et al.: The role of the therapeutic alliance in psychotherapy and pharmacotherapy outcome: findings in the National Institute of Mental Health Treatment of Depression Collaborative Research Program. *J Consult Clin Psychol.* 1996;64:532–539.

Lanius RA, Vermetten E, Lowenstein RJ, et al.: Emotion modulation in PTSD: clinical and neurobiological evidence for a dissociative subtype. *Am J Psychiatry.* 2010; 167:640–647.

Levi P: *If This Is a Man,* 3rd ed. Translated by S Woolf. London: Folio Society, 2003.

Liang B, Williams LM, Siegel JA: Relational outcomes of childhood sexual trauma in female survivors: a longitudinal study. *J Interpers Violence.* 2006;21:42–57.

Lipsitz JD, Fyer AJ, Markowitz JC, Cherry S: An open trial of interpersonal psychotherapy for social phobia. *Am J Psychiatry.* 1999;156:1814–1816.

Lipsitz JD, Markowitz JC: Mechanisms of change in interpersonal psychotherapy. *Clin Psychol Rev.* 2013;33:1134–1147.

Luborsky L, Diguer L, Seligman DA, et al.: The researcher's own therapy allegiances: a "wild card" in comparisons of treatment efficacy. *Clin Psychol Sci Pract.* 1999; 6:95–106.

Markowitz JC, Bleiberg KL, Christos P, Levitan E: Solving interpersonal problems correlates with symptom improvement in interpersonal psychotherapy: preliminary findings. *J Nerv Ment Dis.* 2006;194:15–20.

Markowitz JC, Bleiberg KL, Pessin H, Skodol AE: Adapting interpersonal psychotherapy for borderline personality disorder. *J Ment Health.* 2007;16:103–116.

Markowitz JC, Kocsis JH, Fishman B, Spielman LA, Jacobsberg LB, Frances AJ, Klerman GL, Perry SW: Treatment of depressive symptoms in human immunodeficiency virus-positive patients. *Archives of General Psychiatry.* 1998;55:452–457.

Markowitz JC, Lipsitz J, Milrod BL: A critical review of outcome research on interpersonal psychotherapy for anxiety disorders. *Depress Anxiety.* 2014;31:316–325. Epub Feb. 3, 2014.

Markowitz JC, Meehan KB, Petkova E, et al.: Treatment preferences of psychotherapy patients with chronic PTSD. *J Clin Psychiatry.* 2015a; June 9 [Epub ahead of print].

Markowitz JC, Milrod B, Bleiberg KL, Marshall RD: Interpersonal factors in understanding and treating posttraumatic stress disorder. *J Psychiatr Pract.* 2009;15:133–140.

Markowitz JC, Milrod B: The importance of responding to negative affect in psychotherapies. *Am J Psychiatry.* 2011;168:124–128.

Markowitz JC, Milrod BL: What to do when a psychotherapy fails. *Lancet Psychiatry.* 2015;2:186–190.

Markowitz JC, Patel SR, Balan I, et al.: Towards an adaptation of interpersonal psychotherapy for depressed Hispanic patients. *J Clin Psychiatry.* 2009a;70:214–222.

Markowitz JC, Petkova E, Biyanova T, Ding K, Neria Y: Exploring personality diagnosis stability following acute psychotherapy for chronic posttraumatic stress disorder. *Depress Anxiety.* 2015b;32:919–926.

Markowitz JC, Petkova E, Neria Y, et al.: Is exposure necessary? A randomized clinical trial of interpersonal psychotherapy for PTSD. *Am J Psychiatry.* 2015;172;430–440.

Markowitz JC, Spielman LA, Scarvalone PA, Perry SW: Psychotherapy adherence of therapists treating HIV-positive patients with depressive symptoms. *J Psychother Pract Res.* 2000;9:75–80.

Markowitz JC, Svartberg M, Swartz HA: Is IPT time-limited psychodynamic psychotherapy? *J Psychother Pract Res.* 1998a;7:185–195.

Markowitz JC, Swartz HA: Case formulation in interpersonal psychotherapy of depression. In: *Handbook of Psychotherapy Case Formulation,* 2nd ed. Edited by TD Eells. New York: Guilford Press, 2007:221–250.

Markowitz JC, Weissman MM (Eds.): *Casebook of Interpersonal Psychotherapy.* New York: Oxford University Press, 2012.

Markowitz JC, Weissman MM: IPT: past, present, and future. *Clin Psychol Psychother.* 2012;19:99–105.

Markowitz JC: *Interpersonal Psychotherapy for Dysthymic Disorder.* Washington, DC: American Psychiatric Press, 1998.

Marshall RD, Beebe KL, Oldham M, Zaninelli R: Efficacy and safety of paroxetine treatment for chronic PTSD: a fixed-dose, placebo-controlled study. *Am J Psychiatry.* 2001;158:1982–1988.

McFall M, Fontana A, Raskind M, Rosenheck R: Analysis of violent behavior in Vietnam combat veteran psychiatric inpatients with posttraumatic stress disorder. *J Trauma Stress.* 1999;12:501–517.

McHugh RK, Whitton SW, Peckham AD, Welge JA, Otto MW: Patient preference for psychological vs. pharmacologic treatment of psychiatric disorders: a meta-analytic review. *J Clin Psychiatry.* 2013;74:595–602.

McMillen C, North C, Mosley M, Smith E: Untangling the psychiatric comorbidity of posttraumatic stress disorder in a sample of flood survivors. *Compr Psychiatry.* 2002;43:478–485.

NICE guidelines [CG26]: Post-traumatic stress disorder (PTSD): The management of PTSD in adults and children in primary and secondary care, 2005. At https://www.nice.org.uk/guidance/cg26; accessed May 23, 2015.

Norris FH, Friedman MJ, Watson PJ: 60,000 disaster victims speak: Part II. Summary and implications of the disaster mental health research. *Psychiatry.* 2002;65: 240–260.

North CS, Nixon SJ, Shariat S, et al.: Psychiatric disorders among survivors of the Oklahoma City bombing. *JAMA.* 1999;282:755–762.

Ozer EJ, Best SR, Lipsey TL, Weiss DS: Predictors of posttraumatic stress disorder and symptoms in adults: a meta-analysis. *Psychol Bull.* 2003;129:52–73.

Parsons T: Illness and the role of the physician: a sociological perspective. *Am J Orthopsychiatry.* 1951;21:452–460.

Rauch SL, Shin LM, Phelps EA: Neurocircuitry models of posttraumatic stress disorder and extinction: human neuroimaging research—past, present, and future. *Biol Psychiatry.* 2006;60:376–382.

Ray RD, Webster R: Group interpersonal psychotherapy for veterans with posttraumatic stress disorder: a pilot study. *Int J Group Psychother.* 2010;60:131–140.

Resick PA, Uhlmansiek MO, Clum GA, Galovski TE, Scher CD, Yinong Y-X: A randomized clinical trial to dismantle components of cognitive processing therapy for posttraumatic stress disorder in female victims of interpersonal violence. *J Clin Consult Psychology.* 2008;76:243–258.

Reynolds CF 3rd, Frank E, Perel JM, et al.: Nortriptyline and interpersonal psychotherapy as maintenance therapies for recurrent major depression: a randomized controlled trial in patients older than 59 years. *JAMA.* 1999;281:39–45.

Riggs DS, Byrn CA, Weathers FW, Litz BT: The quality of the intimate relationships of male Vietnam veterans: problems associated with posttraumatic stress disorder. *J Trauma Stress.* 1998;11:87–102.

Robertson M, Rushton P, Batrim D, Moore E, Morris P: Open trial of interpersonal psychotherapy for chronic post-traumatic stress disorder. *Australas Psychiatry.* 2007;15:375–379.

Rounsaville BJ, Chevron ES, Weissman MM, Prusoff BA, Frank E: Training therapists to perform interpersonal psychotherapy in clinical trials. *Compr Psychiatry.* 1986;27:364–371.

Rounsaville BJ, O'Malley S, Foley S, Weissman MM: Role of manual-guided training in the conduct and efficacy of interpersonal psychotherapy for depression. *J Consult Clin Psychol.* 1988;56:681–688.

Rudden MG, Milrod B, Meehan KB, Falkenstrom F: Symptom-specific reflective functioning: incorporating psychoanalytic measures into clinical trials. *J Am Psychoanal Assn.* 2009;57:1473–1478.

Rutimann DD, Meehan KB: Validity of a brief interview for assessing reflective function. *J Am Psychoanal Assn.* 2012;60:577–589.

Sareen J, Cox BJ, Stein MB, Afifi TO, Fleet C, Asmundson GJG: Physical and mental comorbidity, disability, and suicidal behavior associated with posttraumatic stress disorder in a large community sample. *Psychosom Med.* 2007;69:242–248.

Schneier FR, Neria Y, Pavlicova M, et al.: Combined prolonged exposure therapy and paroxetine for PTSD related to the World Trade Center attack: a randomized controlled trial. *Am J Psychiatry.* 2012;169:80–88.

Shalev AY, Freedman S, Peri T, et al.: Prospective study of posttraumatic stress disorder and depression following trauma. *Am J Psychiatry.* 1998;155:630–637.

Shapiro, F: *Eye Movement Desensitization and Reprocessing: Basic Principles, Protocols and Procedures,* 2nd ed. New York: Guilford Press, 2001.

Stein MB, Kessler RC, Heeringa SG, et al.; & Army STARRS collaborators: Prospective longitudinal evaluation of the effect of deployment-acquired traumatic brain injury on posttraumatic stress and related disorders: results from the Army Study to Assess Risk and Resilience in Servicemembers (Army STARRS). *Am J Psychiatry.* 2015;172:1101–1111.

Stewart AL, Greenfield S, Hays RD, et al.: Functional status and well-being of patients with chronic conditions. Results from the Medical Outcomes Study. *JAMA.* 1989; 262:907–913.

Sullivan HS: *The Interpersonal Theory of Psychiatry.* New York: W.W. Norton, 1953.

Wampold BE: *The Great Psychotherapy Debate: Models, Methods, and Findings.* Mahwah, NJ: Lawrence Erlbaum Associates, 2001.

Wang PS, Berglund P, Olfson M, Pincus HA, Wells KB, Kessler RC: Failure and delay in initial treatment contact after first onset of mental disorders in the National Comorbidity Survey Replication. *Arch Gen Psychiatry.* 2005;62:603–613.

Watts BV, Shiner B, Zubkoff L, Carpenter-Song E, Ronconi JM, Coldwell CM: Implementation of evidence-based psychotherapies for posttraumatic stress disorder in VA specialty clinics. *Psychiatric Serv.* 2014;65:648–653.

Weathers FW, Blake DD, Schnurr PP, Kaloupek DG, Marx BP, Keane TM: *The Clinician-Administered PTSD Scale for DSM-5 (CAPS-5).* 2013a. Interview available from the National Center for PTSD at www.ptsd.va.gov.

Weathers FW, Keane TM, Davidson JRT: Clinician-Administered PTSD Scale: a review of the first ten years of research. *Depress Anxiety.* 2001;13:132–156.

Weathers FW, Litz BT, Keane TM, Palmieri PA, Marx BP, Schnurr PP: *The PTSD Checklist for DSM-5 (PCL-5).* 2013. Scale available from the National Center for PTSD at www.ptsd.va.gov.

Weissman MM, Bothwell S: Assessment of social adjustment by patient self-report. *Arch Gen Psychiatry.* 1976;33:1111–1115.

Weissman MM, Kasl SV, Klerman GL: Follow-up of depressed women after maintenance treatment. *Am J Psychiatry.* 1976;133:757–760.

Weissman MM, Markowitz JC, Klerman GL: *Clinician's Quick Guide to Interpersonal Psychotherapy.* New York: Oxford University Press, 2007.

Weissman MM, Markowitz JC, Klerman GL: *Comprehensive Guide to Interpersonal Psychotherapy.* New York: Basic Books, 2000.

Wilfley DE, MacKenzie KR, Welch RR, Ayres VE, Weissman MM: *Interpersonal Psychotherapy for Group.* New York: Basic Books, 2000.

Wilkinson ST, Stefanovics E, Rosenheck RA: Marijuana use is associated with worse outcomes in symptom severity and violent behavior in patients with posttraumatic stress disorder. *J Clin Psychiatry*. 2015;76:1174–1180.

Wisco BE, Marx BP, Miller MW, et al.: Probable posttraumatic stress disorder in the US veteran population according to DSM-5: Results from the National Health and Resilience in Veterans Study. *J Clin Psychiatry* (in press).

Wisco BE, Marx BP, Wolf EJ, Miller MW, Southwick SM, Pietrzak RH: Posttraumatic stress disorder in the US veteran population: results from the National Health and Resilience in Veterans Study. *J Clin Psychiatry*. 2014;75:1338–1346.

John C. Markowitz, M.D., is Professor of Clinical Psychiatry at Columbia University College of Physicians and Surgeons and a Research Psychiatrist at the New York State Psychiatric Institute. Dr. Markowitz is an internationally recognized expert in psychotherapy research who has conducted NIMH- and foundation-funded studies of Interpersonal Psychotherapy (IPT), cognitive behavioral therapies, and medications. He has studied treatments of mood, anxiety, and personality disorders, and has published more than 300 peer-reviewed articles, chapters, and reviews.

abuse by previous therapists, 136
adaptive interpersonal behaviors, supporting, 76
adherence of therapist, 12, 24, 25, 47, 48*f*, 138–40, 142
affect. *See also* anger; emotions/feelings; normalization of affect; sadness; validating feelings
tolerating, 44, 69, 72–73, 141
affective attunement, 8, 24, 54, 72, 89, 146
affective reattunement, 48–50
alexithymia, 33, 49
anger. *See also* normalization of affect
case material, 82–83, 90–93, 95–97, 111–12, 116
expressing, 75, 95–96, 112, 116
validating and normalizing, 64–66, 74, 75, 82–83, 90–93, 97, 111–12, 121, 133
assertion. *See* self-assertion
attachment. *See also* secure attachment
PTSD and, 53–54
attunement. *See* affective attunement; affective reattunement
audiotaping sessions, 138–39
avoidance symptoms, 2–4, 9*t*, 18, 23, 29, 30*t*, 51–53, 61, 72, 80, 86
avoidant personality disorder, 13, 15*t*, 21

Beck, Aaron T., 26
bereavement. *See* complicated grief/ complicated bereavement
blaming. *See also* self-blame
the illness, 33, 38, 40, 42, 62–63, 132
the treatment, 127
the victim, 135
Bleiberg, Kathryn L., vii, 5*t*, 8, 94
borderline personality disorder, 15*t*, 22, 119, 123
breathing exercises, 140

Campanini, R. F., 5*t*, 6–7
chaos, feeling of, 69. *See also* role transition(s)
Cognitive Behavioral Therapy (CBT), x–xi, 3, 22–26, 51–52. *See also* Prolonged Exposure
communication analysis, 71–73
comorbidity, 32, 56, 127, 134–35. *See also under* major depression/major depressive disorder
competence
patient sense of, 52, 86, 88, 104, 125, 126
therapist technical, 12, 142–43
complicated grief/complicated bereavement, 44, 45, 54, 59, 60, 68, 79, 99. *See also* grief
case example, 99–103
confidentiality, 79, 133, 138

dangerousness, 57, 130–33
depression, 70. *See also* complicated grief/
    complicated bereavement; major
    depression/major depressive
    disorder
  assessment of, 139
  as a medical illness, 37–38
  role disputes and, 45
  and self-blame, 33, 38, 40, 42
  and suicide, 130–32
  symptoms of, 37–41, 45
  treatment of, 19, 20*t*, 42–44
detachment, affective/emotional, 3, 4, 31*t*,
    107, 117, 119, 120
direction, regaining a, 45, 69
dissociation, 3, 27, 29, 30*t*, 31*t*, 94,
    108, 126
drug abuse/dependence. *See* substance
    abuse/dependence
duty to warn and duty to protect, 133

eclectic therapy, 132, 140
emotions/feelings. *See also* affect; anger;
    normalization of affect; sadness;
    validating feelings
  eliciting patient's, 40, 65, 69–70, 75–76,
    111, 126, 141, 146
  exploring options for expressing, 70
  learning that they are not dangerous, 49
  life events and, 148
  resisting the temptation to interrupt, 69
  as useful signals about one's
    situation, 149
  verbalizing, 74
exposure therapy/exposure-based
    treatment, xi, 1–3, 47–48. *See
    also* Prolonged Exposure; trauma
    reminders/traumatic reminders
  vs. IPT, 47–48, 48*t*

fault. *See* blaming; self-blame
fear-extinction paradigm, 2, 3
feelings. *See* affect; emotions/feelings
Foa, Edna, 10, 11
formulation, offering the patient a, 39–40,
    44, 59–61
  case material, 81, 88–89, 101–2, 110–11
Frank, Jerome, 65

grief, 39, 68, 105, 149. *See also*
    complicated grief/complicated
    bereavement

habituation, x, 73
Hembree, Elizabeth, 11
history taking, 39, 43, 57, 58. *See also*
    interpersonal inventory
homework, 48*t*, 62, 104, 140, 150
hope, clinical, 42, 59, 61, 64, 67, 85,
    132, 148
hypervigilance, interpersonal, 4, 31*t*,
    50–51, 66, 80, 94

initial phase of IPT, 56. *See also*
    IPT-PTSD: setting the framework
    for treatment; PTSD: diagnosis of;
    symptomatic relief
  goals of, 43–44, 56, 64–67, 67*t*
International Society for Interpersonal
    Psychotherapy, 142, 143
interpersonal aspects and features of
    PTSD, 3–4. *See also specific
    topics*
interpersonal consequences/aftereffects
    of trauma, 50–51
  focusing on, 50
interpersonal deficits, 39, 44–46, 54, 70
interpersonal focus, choice of, 54
interpersonal functioning
  getting an overall sense of patient's, 89
  trauma and, 52
interpersonal interactions in patient's
    daily life, treatment focus
    on, 61–62
interpersonal inventory, 41, 43,
    57–60, 80, 95, 101, 135. *See also*
    history taking
  goals of, 58–59
interpersonal options, recognizing and
    exploring (alternative), 41–42, 44,
    70, 73–77, 83, 85, 91, 96–97, 103–4,
    112–15, 133
interpersonal problem areas, 39. *See also*
    complicated grief/complicated
    bereavement; interpersonal
    deficits; role disputes; role
    transition(s)

IPT (Interpersonal Psychotherapy), x.
  See also specific topics
  background, 36–37
  exposure and, 18, 19*f*
  future of, 145–46
  general competence in, 143
  goals of, 78
  how it works, 51–52, 149–50
  mixing other treatment elements/
    modalities with, 140
  phases of, 43–46. *See also* initial phase
    of IPT; middle phase of IPT;
    termination phase of IPT
  principles of, 37–42, 148
  training in, 142
  what it doesn't do, 150
IPT manuals, vii, xi, 8, 36–37, 47, 68, 79,
  138, 143–45
IPT-PTSD (Interpersonal Psychotherapy
    for posttraumatic stress disorder)
  adapting IPT for PTSD, 47–55
    reasons for, 7–8
  setting the framework for
    treatment, 61–64
  studies of IPT for chronic PTSD, 4, 5*t*,
    6–13, 14*t*–15*t*
    outcomes over time, 13,
      16–17*t*, 18–25
  training in IPT for PTSD, 142–44
IPT-PTSD handout (for patient), 64, 66,
  119, 139, **147–50**
IPT sessions
  audiotaping, 2, 12, 47, 94,
    138–39, 142–44
  scheduling, 44, 63, 129, 138
  structure of, 71–77
    opening gambit, 71
IPT workshops, attending, 143

Kardiner, A., 1
Klerman, Gerald L., 36–38
Krupnick, J. L., 4, 5*t*, 6

life events, ix. *See also* complicated grief/
    complicated bereavement; trauma
  feelings and symptoms as connected
    to, 148

interactions between mood/emotions
    and, 38*f*, 38–42, 65, 76, 78, 148
  IPT and, 7, 37–40, 45, 54, 65, 70, 76,
    78, 148
  and PTSD, 7, 45, 54, 65, 70, 148
Lovell, Karina, 11–12

maintenance treatment, 46, 124–29
major depression/major depressive
    disorder. *See also* depression
  IPT for, xi, 7, 23, 36–41, 47, 105, 127,
    128, 132, 143, 147
  pharmacotherapy for, 37, 42, 43
  PTSD contrasted with, 48–49
  PTSD patients with comorbid
    case material, 79–81, 85–87, 93–97,
      100–102, 105, 118, 120
    and dropout, 18–20, 20*t*, 22, 23
    IPT for, xi, 7, 8, 11, 18, 19, 22, 23, 56,
      68, 134
    prevalence of, 13, 15*t*, 32, 134
    and treatment outcome, xi, 7, 18–20,
      20*t*, 23, 134
  social support and, 41
  symptoms of, 33, 70
    life events and, 37–39
medical model. *See* PTSD: as a medical
    illness; treatability of PTSD
medication. *See also* pharmacotherapy
  deciding whether or not to
    prescribe, 42
middle phase of IPT, 44–46, 68–70,
    78. *See also* IPT sessions;
    specific topics
military PTSD, 29
mistrust. *See also* paranoid personality
    disorder
  of environment, 4, 50, 51, 87, 134
  of people, 4, 87, 96, 134
mood. *See under* life events

9/11 terrorist attacks, 2, 80, 85, 86, 99–105
normalization of affect, 44, 49, 64–66,
    70, 72, 73, 78. *See also*
    anger: validating and normalizing
  case material, 83, 86, 91, 92, 94, 97,
    111–12, 121

options, recognizing and exploring
  (alternative), 73–74, 76–77

paranoid personality disorder, 13, 15t, 21,
  87–88, 93, 134
Parsons, Talcott, 37–38
personality disorders, 13, 21, 22, 87. See
  also avoidant personality disorder;
  paranoid personality disorder
pharmacotherapy
  IPT and, 42, 134–35
  for major depression, 37, 42, 43
  for PTSD, 3, 6, 15t, 22–24, 42–43, 46,
    64, 67t, 127
  efficacy of, 33–35
posttraumatic stress disorder. See PTSD
present, focusing on the, 148
progress note, writing a, 43, 45, 50, 59,
    136, 139, 140, 150
Prolonged Exposure (PE), x
  description and overview of, 2
  effects of IPT vs., 10–13, 12f, 14t–17t,
    18–20, 20t, 21f, 22–26, 134
  effects of Relaxation Therapy vs.,
    10–13, 12f, 14t–17t, 18–20, 20t,
    21f, 22–25
  IPT compared with, 47
  pharmacotherapy combined with, 35
psychodynamic interventions, 140
psychoeducation, 66–67
PTSD (posttraumatic stress disorder), x.
    See also specific topics
  assessment of, 32–33
  diagnosis of, 29, 32–33, 56–61
    DSM5 symptom criteria, 29, 30–31t
  differential diagnosis of, 32
  as a medical illness, 147, 148. See also
    treatability of PTSD
  nature of, 27–35, 147, 148
  prevalence of, 27
  subtypes of, 29
  symptoms of, 3–4, 67
  theories regarding, 2–4
  treatment of, x–xi, 147–48
    practical difficulties the, 130–36
  treatment planning, 33–35

prescriptions: things to do, 138–39
proscriptions: things not to
    do, 139–41
PTSD patients. See also specific topics
  clinical characteristics of, 13, 15t
  demographic characteristics of, 13, 14t
  information therapist will want to
    know about, 148–49
  IPT-PTSD handout for, 139, 147–50
  reassuring them of the treatability of
    PTSD, 33, 38, 48, 57, 67, 147, 148
  treatment preferences and
    disinclinations of, 20, 21f

reflection, 43, 73, 141, 146
reflective function, 53–54
  symptom-specific, 54, 146
reinforcement, providing, 32, 46, 66–67,
    71, 73–76, 126
relationships. See also interpersonal
    inventory
  focus of IPT on current, 52
  renegotiating them into a fairer
    balance, 45, 69–70, 106, 120,
    123, 135
Relaxation Therapy (RT), effects of,
    10–13, 12f, 14t–17t, 18–20, 20t,
    21f, 22–25
reliving trauma, 150
revictimization, 4, 8, 121, **135–36**
risk taking and taking "safe risks," 62, 73,
    75–76, 85, 114, 117, 123, 126, 149
role disputes, 39, 41, 44–46, 54, 58–60,
    68–70, 72, 77, 94, 96, 98, **106–24**,
    135, 142, 149
  case examples, 94–98, 106–24
  finding potential, 58–59
  goal of treating, 45
role play, 41, 44, 69–70, **74–77**, 126, 136, 143
  case material, 84–85, 91–92, 96–97, 103,
    112–13, 115, 118, 121–23
role transition(s), 39, 44, 45, 54, 59, 60,
    66–70, 75, 77, 79, 81, 94, 96, 98,
    117, 124, 135, 140, 149
  case examples, 79–105, 117
  iatrogenic, 51

sadness, 42, 44, 46, 49, 65, 72–73, 126.
    See also complicated grief/
    complicated bereavement; grief
  case material, 86, 102, 105, 111–12
  during termination, 46, 86, 126
"safe risks," taking. *See* risk taking and
    taking "safe risks"
secure attachment, 51, 53, 58–59, 120
self-assertion, 41, 44, 57, 59, 61, 66, 69, 74,
    85, 96, 106, 113, 126, 135
self-blame
  depression and, 33, 38, 40, 42
  PTSD and, 31*t*, 33
  reminding patients that PTSD is not
    their fault, 33, 38, 48, 57, 62–63,
    147, 148
separation, 46. *See also* termination
    phase of IPT
September 11 attacks, 2, 80, 85,
    86, 99–105
sick role, 62, 96
social functioning. *See also* interpersonal
    functioning
  trauma and, 52
social skills, building, xi, 24, 41, 45, 69, 78
social support, xi, 7, 23, 28, 41, 43, 57–59,
    70, 103, 117–18, 127, 131, 145, 150.
    See also interpersonal inventory
  mobilizing/finding potential, 41,
    45–46, 50–53, 58, 150
Spiegel, H., 1
stress-diathesis model, 38
substance abuse/dependence, 12*f*, 15*t*, 19,
    32, 57, 94, 130, **134**
success experiences, 51, 65–66, 68, 71, 74,
    76, 85, 122, 126
suicide/suicidality, 57, 68, **130–32**, 137
  case material, 80, 100, 119
  IPT approach to, 131
supervision, 133–34
support. *See also* social support
  providing, 71
survivor, idea of being a, 66, 77, 126
survivor guilt, 33
sympathy, 40, 59, 64, 71, 73, 75–76,
    101, 150

symptomatic relief, initial, 52, 56,
    64–69
symptoms, life events and, 148
symptom-specific reflective function. *See*
    reflective function

telephone contacts, 137
termination phase of IPT, 46, 48,
    63, **125–28**
  case material, 86, 93–94, 105, 117, 123
  sadness during, 46, 86, 126
  tasks of, 125
    consolidating gains, 46, 125–26
    emotionally acknowledging the end
      of treatment, 126
    next steps, 126–28
thematic continuity, 63, 77–78, 132,
    138, 140
thematic issues, 77–78
therapeutic alliance, 34, 43, 64, 67, 75
therapeutic modalities, 1–3, 15*t*
  blending, 140
  common factors across, 64–65, 65*t*
therapeutic poise, 49, 65, 132–33, 143
therapeutic stance, 42–43, 77–78, 88,
    128, 131
therapists
  abuse by previous, 59, 136
  information they will want to
    know, 148–49
  technical competence, 12, 142–43
therapist's adherence to treatment. *See*
    adherence of therapist
therapy, previous
  inquiring about, 43, 59, 136
  portion of PTSD patients who have had
    various types of, 15*t*
therapy sessions. *See* IPT sessions
time-limited approach to therapy,
    42–44, 65
  advantages of, 34
transgression, 70, 83, 121. *See also* abuse
    by previous therapists
trauma, ix, xx. *See also* life events;
    September 11 attacks
  defined, ix

trauma (*Cont.*)
  interpersonal aftereffects of, focusing
    on the, 50
  types of, 27–29
trauma reminders/traumatic reminders,
    x–xi, 22, 23, 30*t*, 48*t*, 48*f*, 51–52,
    146. *See also* exposure therapy/
    exposure-based treatment
  not encouraging exposure to, 22, 23,
    52, 78, 140
treatability of PTSD, reassuring patient of
    the, 33, 38, 48, 57, 67, 147, 148. *See
    also* PTSD: as a medical illness

treatment progress, ratings to assess,
    139, 150
treatment sessions. *See* IPT sessions

validating feelings, 66, 70, 72, 76. *See
    also* anger: validating and
    normalizing
violence, 132–33. *See also* suicide

war trauma, 29
Weissman, Myrna M., vii, 36–38, 143
World Trade Center attack. *See*
    September 11 attacks